Think Like a
Psychiatrist
40 Cases

SECOND EDITION

UNDERSTANDING PSYCHIATRIC MEDICINES

40 Cases

Think Like a Psychiatrist

SECOND EDITION

Leslie Lundt, M.D.

PESI®

Eau Claire, Wisconsin

2009

Printed in the United States of America

Published by PESI, LLC

The tables used throughout the book were designed by Jana Bassett
Cover design by Sean Fields

Disclaimers

Think Like a Psychiatrist: 40 Cases is intended solely for educational and informational purposes and not as medical advice. Please consult a medical or health professional if you have any questions about your health.

Dr. Lundt has received research support from Cephalon, Eli Lilly, Forest, GSK, Merck, Organon, Ortho-McNeil, Pfizer, Pharmacia, Sepracor, Shire, and Targacept. She has participated as a consultant or speaker for BMS, Cephalon, Eli Lilly, Forest, Genesis Pharma, GSK, Janssen, Orphan Medical, Organon, Pfizer, Sanofi-Aventis, Sepracor, Shire BioChem, Solvay, Takeda and Wyeth.

I have done my best to make sure all Internet Addresses in this book were active and appropriate when this book went to press. However, the author and the publisher have no control over and assume no liability for the material available on those Internet sites or on other Web sites they may link to. Any comments or suggestions for additional resources can be sent by e-mail to leslie@leslielundt.com.

All of the patients presented in this book are completely fictional. Any similarities to real people are entirely coincidental. The opinions expressed herein are those of Leslie Lundt.

PESI, LLC strives to obtain knowledgeable authors and faculty for its publications and seminars. The clinical recommendations contained herein are the result of extensive author research and review. Obviously, any recommendations for patient care must be held up against individual circumstances at hand. To the best of our knowledge any recommendations included by the author or faculty reflect currently accepted practice. However, these recommendations cannot be considered universal and complete. The authors and publisher repudiate any responsibility for unfavorable effects that result from information, recommendations, undetected omissions or errors. Professionals using this publication should research other original sources of authority as well.

For information on this and other PESI books, audio and
video recordings, please call 800-844-8260 or
visit our website at www.pesi.com

PESI, LLC, PO Box 1000, 3839 White Avenue, Eau Claire, Wisconsin 54702

Dedication

To Mick, Jackson, Jenny, Pierce, Blaine

From First Edition
To Our Readers

The people who attend our seminars and workshops are health care providers who counsel and guide the treatment of thousands of patients with a variety of mental health disorders. They like the information we provide, but from their questions we could tell they needed something more. They wanted to see real-life examples of how the principles of diagnosis and treatment are applied by psychiatrists. In short, they wanted a case book.

For months we sifted through the records of our patients looking for common threads that we could weave into a set of illustrations without encroaching on their privacy. We obscured or deleted identifying details, combined features from several cases, and made up outrageous names to help the reader associate each case with its problem.

Our resulting work, *40 Cases*, is by no means comprehensive, but we think it gives the reader an excellent guide that can be useful in dealing with virtually any mental health disorder encountered in an outpatient or client setting.

Put the information in *40 Cases* to work for you—and let us know what you'd like to see in the next edition.

Second Edition

One of the many delightful (and challenging) things about practicing medicine is that things never stay the same. Since the first edition of *40 Cases*, several new medications have been approved and brought to market. Some are not much different than what was previously available (Luvox CR, Seroquel XR), others are active metabolites of older medications (Pristiq and Invega), and still others involve a new drug delivery system (EmSam, Vyvanse, Vivitrol, Daytrana). One that is truly different is Chantix which has been enormously helpful in getting people to stop smoking (with a little controversy thrown into the mix).   Medications mentioned in the first edition that never made it to the public include Acomplia and Sparlon. Savella has just been approved and Nuvigil, although approved, has not yet hit the shelves. Web sites have come and gone and new books have been published.

Another delightful (and challenging) change is that Nancy Nadolski, my dear friend and co-author of the first edition has moved from psychiatry into full-time motherhood. Throughout my career I have been blessed with wonderful colleagues, often I speak of "our" experience.

Many of the cases in this edition have thus been revised to reflect all of the changes in our world.

Contents

Dedication v

To Our Readers...vi

Anxiety Disorders

Case 1: Annie Airscare 2

Case 2: Nervous Nellie 6

Case 3: Pamela Panic 9

Case 4: Petunia Hair Puller 13

Case 5: Rhonda Rituals 16

Case 6: Traumatized Teresa 19

Attention Disorders

Case 7: Distracted David 23

Case 8: Ned NoMeds 27

Case 9: Hyper Harry 32

Case 10: Restless Rita 35

Case 11: Tom Sawyer's Twin 38

Cognitive Disorders

Case 12: Forgetful Fabian 42

Eating Disorders

Case 13: Anorexic Angela 47

Mood Disorders

Case 14: Amelia Airheart 51

Case 15: Billy Bully 55

Case 16: Daniel Darkmood 59

Case 17: Brooke Blue 62

Case 18: Frustrated Fred 65

Case 19: Polarized Perry 69

Case 20: Herman Heartache 72

Case 21: Lonely Loni 75

Case 22: Marilyn Moodswinger—1 78

Case 23: Marilyn Moodswinger—2 81

Case 24: Mike Moody 84

Case 25: Paula. Period. 87

Case 26: Peter Pendulum—1 90

Case 27: Peter Pendulum—2 94

Case 28: Peter Pendulum—3 96

Case 29: Sobbing Sylvia 98

Case 30: Wanda Worrywart 101

Psychotic Disorders

Case 31: Psychotic Peggy 106

Case 32: Randy's Racket 109

Sleep Disorders

Case 33: Coach Camille 113

Case 34: Florence Nightingnurse 117

Case 35: Jetlag Jerry 121

Case 36: Sleepless Suzy 124

Case 37: Nigel Nightowl 128

Case 38: Warren A. Widower 132

Substance Abuse Disorders

Case 39: Al Kohall 136

Case 40: Nick Nicotine 140

Reviewers **145**

Abbreviations and Acronyms **146**

Index **147**

Tables

Anxiolytics (Benzodiazepines) 5

Drug Interactions 25

ADHD Drugs 30

Medications to Treat Alzheimer's 45

Therapy Types 54

Mood Stabilizers and Laboratory Monitoring 58

Antipsychotics Approved for Bipolar Disorder 68

Weight Gain Liabilities of Common Psychiatric Medications 93

Antidepressants (non-SSRI) 104

Common Sleep Aids 116

Caffeine Content 120

Sleep Diary 127

Medications to try for Alcoholism 139

Comparison of Nicotine Replacement Products 143

Anxiety Disorders

Case of

Annie Airscare

Annie Airscare is a 26-year-old single female who presents with intense fears related to flying. She has worked for the same company in one location since graduating from college four years ago. She recently has been awarded a promotion that requires her to travel out of state up to four times a year.

On her first flight she recalls experiencing shortness of breath, nausea, heart palpitations, chest pain, feelings of choking and thinking she was going to die. The second time this happened her nurse practitioner checked her for heart problems and everything physical checked out just fine. Each time she gets on an airplane the symptoms return with varying intensity and if at all possible she prefers driving to flying. "It only happens when I fly." Annie recognizes this fear is excessive and unreasonable but she cannot control it.

Family History: Grandmother had "nerves."

Medical History: Negative

Substance Use: 1 glass of wine 2-3 times a week. Coffee 2-3 cups day.

Medications: Birth control pills, multivitamin

What do you do?

While she has been able to control her phobia by limiting her flying, Annie is now faced with a schedule that demands getting on an airplane in order to perform her job.

> **Diagnosis: Specific phobia, situational type**

Options

1. Cognitive Behavior Therapy (CBT)

Cognitive behavior therapies have shown to be very successful in treating panic. Cognitive behavior treatment takes into account the idea that patients become alarmed by the sensations of their body such as shortness of breath or dizziness. With therapy the client learns to understand the sensations and recognize that they are harmless and can be controlled. Exposure to external cues in a safe environment teaches people how to view panic attacks differently and develop ways to reduce anxiety with relaxation techniques and coping strategies.

2. Treat with antidepressants

The class of medications called SSRIs has been shown to be very effective in treating panic disorder. Paxil (paroxetine), Prozac (fluoxetine), and Zoloft (sertraline) all have FDA approval for panic, but Celexa (citalopram), Lexapro (escitalopram), and Luvox (fluvoxamine) may also work. These medications are not rescue medications and can take up to 2 weeks for a response and 4-8 weeks for remission. They require titrating to a dose that manages the symptoms with few or no side effects. Patients need to be seen weekly after starting on these medications to minimize the risk of increased anxiety at the beginning of treatment.

3. Treat with benzodiazepines

Xanax (alprazolam) and Klonopin (clonazepam) are benzodiazepines that are approved by the FDA for panic disorder. Unlike SSRIs, these medicines can be used to rescue the patient from the immobilizing panic symptoms. How soon the medication gets into the brain and how long it stays active in the body help determine which benzodiazepine is the right medication for the problem at hand.

4. Treat with beta blocker

Inderal (propranolol), Tenormin (atenolol), and other beta blockers have been shown to be effective in blocking symptoms such as racing heartbeat, chest pain, tremor, and other physical symptoms of anxiety.

My Choice

Because Annie's symptoms are limited to flying, she does not need a 24/7 medication regimen like an SSRI. Over time, intense cognitive behavior therapy may resolve Annie's anxiety. In the meantime we will add a short-acting benzodiazepine like Xanax 0.5 mg approximately one hour before her flights. We will coach Annie to have a practice session with the Xanax before her actual flight to establish timing and an effective dose. We will also remind Annie that these medications and alcohol do not mix, so she cannot have a cocktail on the plane.

Annie is well educated and motivated. This is a good time to reinforce the importance of exercise as a stress reliever and ask her to hold off on coffee 2-3 days before taking her flight.

Likely side effects

Benzodiazepines can create sedation as well as motor and cognitive side effects such as memory lapses. Cognitive behavior therapy takes time, a good therapist, and a strong commitment to the sessions.

Risks

Benzodiazepines can be addicting, but Annie is at a low risk since she has no history of substance abuse. The side effects of benzodiazepines make driving risky, and performance of other tasks requiring a high degree of vigilance may be adversely affected.

Resources

Web Sites

National Institutes of Mental Health
Anxiety Disorders
www.nimh.nih.gov/publicat/anxiety.cfm

Anxiety Disorders Association of America
The Anxiety Disorders Guide
www.anxiety-disorders.net/treatment.html

Books/CDs

Fly Without Fear: Guided Meditations for a Relaxing Flight
K.R. Edstrom
Soft Stone Publishing, 2008

Fear Without Flying
Duane Brown
New Harbinger Publications, 1996

The Fearless Flyer's Handbook
Debbie Seaman
Ten Speed Press, 1999

Fearless Flyer: How to Fly in Comfort Without Trepidation
Cherry Hartman, Julie Huffaker, Julie Sheldon Huffaker, Nancy Coffelt
Eighth Mountain Press, 1995

Fly Without Fear or Stress: Learning Mindfulness and Meditation
Eugene Barron
iUniverse, 2002

Anxiolytics (Benzodiazepines)

Agent	Approved Indications	Pharmacokinetic Parameters		
		Approved Oral Adult Dosage Range (mg/d)	Onset (PO)	t½
Ativan (lorazepam)	anxiety; preoperative sedation	1-8 1-4 mg single dose	fast	short
Klonopin (clonazepam)	seizure disorders; panic disorder	0.5-2	moderate	long
Librium (chlordiazepoxide)	anxiety, alcohol withdrawal; preoperative sedation	5-100 25-50 mg single dose	fast	long
Serax (oxazepam)	anxiety disorders; alcohol withdrawal	30-120	slow	short
Tranxene (clorazepate)	anxiety, seizure disorders; alcohol withdrawal	15-60	very fast	long
Valium (diazepam)	anxiety, alcohol withdrawal; muscle spasm; preoperative sedation; status epilepticus	2-40 2-10 mg single dose	very fast	long
Xanax (alprazolam)	anxiety disorders; panic disorder	0.25-4.0	fast	intermediate

Adapted from CNS News Special Edition, December 2004

Case of

Nervous Nellie

Nellie, a 55-year-old divorced female, is referred by her daughter. She has a lifelong history of "bad nerves," which she describes as being always on edge and fearing the worst, suffering from impaired concentration, difficulty sleeping and frequent aches and pains. Nellie says that she cannot remember ever being relaxed; her mantra is "what if?"

Family History: Daughter has been unable to tolerate Celexa, Zoloft, or Paxil.

Medical History: Hysterectomy 10 years ago

Substance Use: Smokes 1 PPD   Medications: Premarin

What do you do?

Nellie has had many interpersonal difficulties due to her anxiety. She feels that it was the main contributor that led to her divorce. She has never presented for treatment because she is fearful of medications after seeing a television show depicting the horrors of antidepressants.

Diagnosis: Generalized Anxiety Disorder (GAD)

Options

1. No medications—Cognitive Behavior Therapy (CBT) only

2. Treat with benzodiazepines

Benzos can be helpful for acute episodes of anxiety, but many psychiatrists are reluctant to prescribe them for chronic anxiety because of issues of tolerance and dependence.

3. Treat with SSRIs

Lexapro and Paxil are FDA approved for treating Generalized Anxiety Disorder (GAD), and there is clinical data to support the use of other SSRIs for treating GAD as well.

4. Treat with BusPar

BusPar is a non-benzodiazepine anti-anxiety agent. It works through the serotonin system, but it is not an antidepressant. It does not work well for panic attacks, but has good success in treating GAD. BusPar has an undeserved reputation as being ineffective, mostly because when it was introduced doctors hoped it would replace benzodiazepines. BusPar is very different from benzos. Unlike benzos, BusPar takes a week or two to take effect and does not work as a rescue medication.

5. Treat with SNRI

Effexor XR and Cymbalta are other antidepressants that are FDA approved for Generalized Anxiety Disorder (GAD). They works on both serotonin and norepinephrine.

My choice

We have had good success with SSRIs, Effexor XR and BusPar in patients with Generalized Anxiety Disorder (GAD). In Nellie's case, she has preconceived negative feelings about SSRIs due to her daughter's experience and what she has seen on television. Often this translates into poor compliance and decreased ability to tolerate side effects.

My choice for Nellie would be Effexor XR. It works well in GAD and may be beneficial in relieving her aches and pains. We will start at 37.5 mg each morning for one week and then increase to 75 mg daily for one week. Most of our patients require at least 150 mg daily.

BusPar is another good choice and is available in generic form. We would not recommend benzos as this is a chronic condition that will likely require lifelong treatment.

Psychotherapy, relaxation training and minimizing caffeine use are also important.

Next we need to work on Nellie's nicotine dependence.

Likely side effects

Effexor XR: nausea and anxiety, which can be minimized by starting with a low dose and taking the medication with food.

BusPar: sedation and dizziness.

Risks

All antidepressants can initially increase anxiety and aggravate an already depressed mood. In some people, these feelings may trigger homicidal or suicidal ideation. This is quite uncommon, but patients starting on antidepressants need to be monitored closely—especially in the first month of treatment. Effexor XR can cause an increase in blood pressure. It is very important to warn patients not to stop their antidepressants suddenly, or symptoms of a nasty discontinuation syndrome may result.

Resources

Web Sites

Anxiety Disorders Association of America
www.adaa.org/gettingHelp/AnxietyDisorders/GAD.asp
General information about anxiety disorders

Anxiety Disorders Association of America
Improving the Diagnosis & Treatment of Generalized Anxiety Disorder: A
Dialogue Between Mental Health Professionals and Primary Care Physicians
www.adaa.org/bookstore/Brochures/GAD_adaa.pdf
Free book via download

Books

Worried Sick: the Exaggerated Fear of Physical Illness
Fredric Neuman, MD
Simon and Brown, 2008

Treating Generalized Anxiety Disorder: Evidence-Based Strategies, Tools, and Techniques
Jayne L Rygh and William C. Sanderson
Guilford Press, 2004

Treating Health Anxiety: A Cognitive-Behavioral Approach
Steven Taylor and Gordon Asmundson
Guilford Press, 2004

Generalized Anxiety Disorder: Advances in Research and Practice
Richard Heimberg, Cynthia Turk, and Douglas Mennin
Guilford Press, 2004

Overcoming Generalized Anxiety Disorder - Client Manual: A Relaxation, Cognitive Restructuring, and Exposure-Based Protocol for the Treatment of GAD (Best Practices for Therapy)
John White
New Harbinger Publications, 2008

Case of

Pamela Panic

Pamela, a 35-year-old married female, is referred by her cardiologist. She began having "attacks" three months ago. During these 15-minute episodes she feels like she is going crazy along with shortness of breath, a choking sensation, rapid heartbeat, shaking and sweating. The first attack landed her in the emergency room. There was no evidence of a heart attack, which is what she feared. She refused to believe that there was "nothing wrong" with her and saw a cardiologist as an outpatient. Her medical workup is completely negative. These attacks are unprovoked and happen several times weekly.

Family History: Sister on Prozac for depression

Medical History: None   Substance Use: Occasional glass of wine, no caffeine

Medications: Birth control pills

What do you do?

Rule out depression and other anxiety disorders by taking a careful history. Pamela's only psychiatric symptoms are these brief episodes, which happen without warning. She is now beginning to fear that they will escalate.

Diagnosis: Panic disorder without agoraphobia

Options

1. No medications—Cognitive Behavior Therapy (CBT) only

CBT has been shown to be extremely effective if done well for at least 12 consecutive weeks.

2. Treat with benzodiazepines

Benzos such as Xanax (alprazolam) and Klonopin (clonazepam) work almost immediately for the symptoms of panic. Many psychiatrists prefer longer acting agents such as Klonopin and Xanax XR because there may be less risk of abuse. However, Ativan (lorazepam) can be a superior choice—if you take it sublingually (under the tongue) it begins to work almost immediately, which can be handy in the midst of an attack.

3. Treat with SSRIs

Prozac (fluoxetine), Zoloft (sertraline), and Paxil (paroxetine) are approved by the FDA for treating panic disorder. The other SSRIs—Celexa (citalopram), Lexapro (escitalopram) and Luvox (fluvoxamine)—also work. These medicines can take several weeks to be effective. There is also a side effect burden: sometimes they can increase anxiety at the beginning of treatment.

4. Treat with tricyclic antidepressants (TCAs)

Tofranil (imipramine) and Norpramin (desipramine) were the mainstays of panic treatment years ago. They are seldom used now because of the risk of lethal overdose and a generally higher risk of uncomfortable side effects.

5. Treat with MAO Inhibitors

Likewise, Nardil (phenelzine) and Parnate (tranylcypromine) were commonly used in the past to treat panic disorder. Although effective, they have fallen out of favor due to fear of drug interactions, orthostatic hypotension and mandatory dietary restrictions.

6. Treat with Beta Blockers

Beta blockers such as Inderal (propranolol) or Tenormin (atenolol) can be helpful for the physical symptoms of anxiety such as rapid heartbeat, sweating and tremor. They do not help with the psychological symptoms of anxiety.

My Choice

The patient's preference is especially important in treating anxiety disorders. Often anxiety patients have strong feelings about cognitive therapy vs medications. I honor this preference whenever possible.

If the patient prefers medication treatment, start with an SSRI. In Pamela's case, her sister has done well on Prozac for her depression, so this would be a logical medicine to start. I always start SSRIs at low doses to minimize the chance of anxiety-like side effects, 5-10 mg each morning. Prozac would be titrated up until her symptoms disappear. Simultaneously, I might add Klonopin 0.25 mg twice daily and increase to 1.0 mg as necessary.

After several weeks on the combination of Klonopin and Prozac, slowly taper Pamela off of the low doses of Klonopin and keep her on Prozac alone.

Another option would be to add Inderal to manage her physical symptoms, remembering that this alone would not help with her psychic anxiety.

Likely side effects

Benzodiazepines: sedation.

SSRIs: GI side effects, anxiety at the beginning, sexual side effects often persist.

Inderal: fatigue.

Risks

Benzodiazepines can be abused although this is unlikely in patients without a history of addictive disorders.

SSRIs bring about mood changes and anxiety that may trigger thoughts of homicide or suicide. This is quite uncommon, but patients newly started on antidepressants need to be monitored closely—especially in the first month of treatment.

Beta Blockers can trigger asthma attacks and should not be used in patients with a history of breathing problems. Similarly, since beta blockers can worsen diabetes, they should also be avoided in these patients.

Resources

Web Sites

Anxiety Disorders Association of America
www.adaa.org/gettingHelp/AnxietyDisorders/Panicattack.asp

Anxiety coach
www.anxietycoach.com/

the Anxiety Panic Internet Resource (Tapir)
www.algy.com/anxiety/panic.php

Books

Surviving Panic Disorder: What You Need to Know
Stuart Shipko
Authorhouse, 2003

The Anxiety & Phobia Workbook
Edmund J. Bourne
New Harbinger Publications, 2005

The Relaxation & Stress Reduction Workbook
Martha Davis, et al
New Harbinger Publications, 2008

Practice Guidelines

Treatment of Patients with Panic Disorder, Second Edition
http://www.psychiatryonline.com/pracGuide/pracGuideChapToc_9.aspx

Case of

Petunia Hair Puller

Petunia, a 12-year-old girl, is brought in by her mother because she is pulling out her eyelashes. This began at age 9 when she changed schools. Upon interview, Petunia states that she also pulls out the hair of her dog, but is afraid to pull her own head hair because it would make her look "ugly."

She describes feeling ashamed and guilty after the eyelash and dog hair pulling but denies any other symptoms.

Family History: Mother has depression and takes Zoloft. Paternal aunt also on antidepressants, not sure which one.

Medical History: Negative

Medications: Vitamins

What do you do?

Is medication treatment necessary in this case? The first step should be cognitive behavior therapy to help Petunia deal with the anxiety which leads to the pulling and also to deal with the resultant shame and guilt following the episodes.

She successfully completes therapy and stops pulling. Her symptoms return when she begins high school at age 14, but now she is pulling the hair on her head that has resulted in a cosmetically distressing bald spot the size of her palm. She returns to your office in tears.

Now what?

She is referred to her original therapist, but her symptoms are now causing her significant distress.

Diagnosis: Trichotillomania

Options

1. No medications—Cognitive Behavior Therapy (CBT) only

Petunia is distressed by her appearance and wishes to be "normal" again. Because she seems to be highly motivated to change, resuming CBT without medications is certainly an option.

2. Treat with Obsessive Compulsive Disorder (OCD) medication such as an SSRI

The only medications approved in children and adolescents for OCD are Luvox (fluvoxamine), Prozac (fluoxetine), Zoloft (sertraline), and Anafranil (clomipramine). Luvox (the brand name, which has been discontinued in the U.S.) is an SSRI, a lesser-known relative of Prozac, Zoloft, Paxil, Celexa, and Lexapro. Luvox CR (Controlled Release) is a newer preparation of fluvoxamine, but is not FDA approved for use in children. Theoretically, any of these serotonergic agents should decrease OCD symptoms. There is some controversy whether or not trichotillomania is a variant of OCD, but the literature and experience supports the theory that SSRIs can alleviate hair pulling. One may make the argument to start Petunia on Zoloft, as her mother's depression has responded well to this agent. I recommend starting all anxious patients on very low doses of these medications as there is a risk of anxiety as a side effect.

3. Give a benzodiazepine for anxiety

Benzodiazepines are helpful for short-term treatment of anxiety and can be taken as needed. However, they are not approved by the FDA for adolescents and there is little data to support their efficacy in treating hair pulling.

My Choice

Zoloft for Petunia's pulling. Start very low—half of a 25 mg tablet. Gradually increase daily dose by 12.5 mg each week until she improves. The maximum dose recommended by the FDA is 200 mg daily.

Since compulsive hair pulling is frequently associated with other obsessive compulsive spectrum issues, Petunia should be screened for OCD, tics and ADHD.

Likely side effects

Zoloft: Nausea, stomach upset, and diarrhea, which usually improve with time.

Risks

SSRIs such as Zoloft are rarely associated with suicidal/homicidal ideation even without pre-existing depression. Petunia needs to be monitored closely during the first several weeks of treatment. A detailed risk/benefit discussion with Petunia's parents is necessary.

Resources

Web Sites

The Trichotillomania Learning Center. A comprehensive and up-to-date resource. There is even a dedicated portion of the sites for children and teens.
www.trich.org/about/for-kids-teens.html

Books

The Hair Pulling "Habit" and You
A workbook for young people with trichotillomania.
S. Vavrichek, R. Golomb and E. Condon-Douglas
Writer's Coop of Greater Washington, 2000

What's Happening to My Child? A Guide for Parents of Hair Pullers.
Cheryn Salazar. A terrific resource for parents of hair pullers.
Available through www.trich.org or www.cheryn.com

Help for Hair Pullers: Understanding and Coping with Trichotillomania.
Nancy J. Keuthen, Ph.D, Dan J. Stein, Gary A. Christenson
New Harbinger Publications, 2001

Stay Out of My Hair!
Parenting your Child with Trichotillomania
Suzanne Mouton-Odum and Ruth Golomb
Goldum Publishing, 2009

Trichotillomania: An ACT-enhanced Behavior Therapy Approach Workbook (Treatments That Work)
Douglas W Woods and Michael P Twohig
Oxford University Press, 2008

Videos

Bad Hair Life. A documentary film by Jennifer Raikes. Available through Fanlight at (800) 937-4113 or www.trich.org

Case of

Rhonda Rituals

Rhonda, a 29-year-old secretary, is referred by her employee assistance counselor. She notes that since her son was born two years ago that she has become more of a perfectionist. Every morning before work she has an elaborate ritual of showering for 11 minutes, brushing her hair 133 strokes, and tapping the bathroom sink four times. She acknowledges that this takes a lot of time and that her husband wonders why she must use all of the hot water.

Her job performance has suffered recently as she must count the paper clips in her desk drawer every hour. The family's medical bills have increased dramatically due to Rhonda's fear that her two-year-old son has undiagnosed cancer. Reassurance from her pediatrician does not stop her worries. Thinking about her son keeps her from falling asleep at night.

Family History: Father has had anxiety in the past

Medical History: None   Substance Use: None

Medications: None

What do you do?

Rhonda's functioning has taken a turn for the worst since her son was born. She has obsessions (intrusive thoughts) and compulsions. OCD is often precipitated by pregnancy and childbirth as fears of contamination are triggered by the new experience of caring for a newborn.

Diagnosis: Obsessive Compulsive Disorder (OCD)

Options

1. No medications—refer for cognitive behavior therapy

CBT can be helpful for OCD but it can be difficult to find a qualified therapist. Rhonda has strong feelings about her new role as mother and caretaker that could be contributing to her symptoms.

2. Treat with SSRIs

Prozac (fluoxetine), Paxil (paroxetine), Zoloft (sertraline) and Luvox CR (fluvoxamine) are all approved by the FDA for OCD. Many patients find Prozac activating and Paxil sedating. SSRIs can take several weeks to work on obsessions and compulsions and often require higher doses than are typically used in depression.

3. Treat with Anafranil

Anafranil (clomipramine) is an interesting compound—a combination of tricyclic antidepressant and SSRI. Many psychiatrists believe that Anafranil is more effective than SSRIs but studies show that it may have more side effects. An advantage is that blood levels of the medication may help guide dosing.

4. Off-label strategies

Because OCD can be resistant to traditional treatments, many other medications have been tried including the atypical antipsychotics, other antidepressants, anticonvulsants, naltrexone, acamprosate, and even opiate pain medication.

My Choice

I recommend a combination of psychotherapy and medication for OCD. It can take months for medication to have a positive effect, so CBT may help Rhonda stay in treatment and manage her symptoms.

Even though Anafranil can cause significant side effects, it is my first choice for OCD in a medically healthy patient. It is sedating and might help with initial insomnia. I would begin Rhonda with 25 mg QHS and very slowly titrate her dose upward.

If side effects became a problem, consider a switch to an SSRI such as Paxil or Prozac.

Likely side effects

Anafranil can cause TCA side effects such as sedation, dry mouth, weight gain and orthostatic hypotension (a decrease in blood pressure when you stand up). Anafranil can also cause cardiac arrhythmias so regular blood levels and EKGs are prudent. SSRI side effects may include sexual dysfunction and anxiety.

Risks

Even though we are using Anafranil as an anti-OCD medication, it may rarely precipitate suicidal or homicidal behavior. As with any antidepressant, careful monitoring is necessary—especially in the first several weeks or after a dosage change. Anafranil can be lethal in overdose.

Resources

Web Sites

> OCD Foundation
> www.ocfoundation.org
>
> Madison Institute of Medicine
> Obsessive Compulsive Information Center
> www.miminc.org/aboutocic.asp

Books

> *The OCD Workbook: Your Guide to Breaking Free from Obsessive-Compulsive Disorder* (Second Edition)
> Bruce M Hyman, PhD and Cherry Pedrick, RN
> New Harbinger Publications, 2005
>
> *Brain Lock: Free Yourself from Obsessive-Compulsive Behavior*
> Jeffrey M Schwartz, MD
> Harper Perennial, 1997
>
> *Loving Someone with OCD: Help for You and Your Family*
> Karen J. Landsman, Kathleen M. Rupertus, and Cherry Pedrick
> New Harbinger Publications, 2005
>
> *Essential Psychopharmacology: The Prescriber's Guide*
> Stephen Stahl, MD
> Cambridge University Press, 2009

Practice Guidelines

> www.psychiatryonline.com/pracGuide/pracGuideTopic_10.aspx

Case of

Traumatized Teresa

Teresa is a 31-year-old single woman who was a witness to a violent murder. She helped the police in their investigation and was considered an ideal witness. For the past three months since the arrest, she has begun to have recurrent nightmares that carry over into vivid memories of the crime. She is easily startled during the day, and her work is suffering due to poor concentration. For the past two months her friends have been complaining that she is avoiding them and drinking too much. She states she feels guilty for not being able to do more to stop the murder and is afraid something like this is going to happen to her again.

Family History: Dad is recovering alcoholic

Medical History: Appendectomy

Substance Use: 3-4 beers day

Medications: Oral Contraceptives

What do you do?

Teresa has experienced an event outside the range of human experience that would evoke extreme distress in most individuals. Symptoms usually appear within three months of the trauma, but can be delayed for months, or even years.

Diagnosis: Post Traumatic Stress Disorder (PTSD)

Options

1. No medications—refer for psychotherapy and cognitive behavior therapy

Psychotherapy is at the heart of treatment for PTSD. The process of therapy is to reexamine the traumatic event and the patient's response to it. Education about the disease and recognition of cues or situations that trigger symptoms are invaluable. If available, a support group for PTSD is recommended.

2. Treat with SSRIs

Selective serotonin reuptake inhibitors (SSRIs) have the broadest range of efficacy to reduce PTSD symptoms. While Paxil (paroxetine) and Zoloft (sertraline) have specific FDA approval for PTSD, all SSRIs have been shown to treat the depression and anxiety symptoms related to the disorder.

3. Treat with benzodiazepines

Klonopin (clonazepam) and Xanax (alprazolam) are effective against anxiety, insomnia and irritability, but they should be used with great caution because of the high frequency of comorbid substance dependence in patients with PTSD.

4. Treat with sedating antidepressant

Though not effective as a primary treatment for mood or anxiety, Desyrel (trazodone) can augment the antidepressant effects of SSRIs by promoting sleep through its sedative properties.

5. Try off-label medications

Though not approved by the FDA, Topamax (topiramate) and Minipress (prazosin) are used by experienced psychopharmacologists to treat the disabling symptoms of PTSD, especially nightmares.

My Choice

Must address her alcohol abuse as Teresa has a family history of alcoholism. Many patients with PTSD turn to substance abuse to self-treat the symptoms of anxiety and insomnia.

Psychotherapy needs to include thorough education about the disorder and enrollment in a local PTSD group.

Start Zoloft 12.5 mg and titrate in weekly intervals to treat the depression, anxiety and hypervigilance. Zoloft can help relieve symptoms and help the patient concentrate on therapy. Also perhaps start Desyrel for sleep (25 mg to 600 mg dosage range).

A sedating benzodiazepine can also help with sleep, but Teresa has a family history of alcoholism and is abusing alcohol herself, so there is a definite risk of dependence and addiction.

Likely side effects

When starting a patient on an SSRI like Zoloft, close monitoring is important in the first several weeks to watch for risk of agitation and suicidal ideation. Desyrel can cause sedation into the next day.

Risks

Teresa needs support to continue therapy. Symptoms of PTSD can occur for up to 10 years after the precipitating event.

Resources

Web Sites

National Institute of Mental
Healthwww.nimh.nih.gov/topics/ptsd.shtml

Anxiety Disorders Association of
Americawww.adaa.org/GettingHelp/AnxietyDisorders/PTSD.asp

The American Academy of Experts in Traumatic Stress
www.aaets.org/index.html

Books

I Can't Get over It: A Handbook for Trauma Survivors
Aphrodite Mataskis
New Harbinger Publications, 1996

*The Post Traumatic Stress Disorder Source Book: A Guide to Healing,
Recovery, and Growth* (Second Edition)
Glenn R. Schiraldi
McGraw Hill, 2009

*PTSD Workbook: Simple, Effective Techniques for Overcoming Traumatic
Stress Symptoms*
Mary Beth Williams and Soili Poijula
New Harbinger Publications, 2002

*Effective Treatments for PTSD: Practice Guidelines from the International
Society of Traumatic Stress Studies*
Edna B. Foa
Guilford Press, 2004

Practice Guidelines

www.psychiatryonline.com/pracGuide/pracGuideTopic_11.aspx

Attention Disorders

Case of

Distracted David

David, a 31-year-old CPA, returns to the office after a three-week trial of Strattera (atomoxetine). He was diagnosed with ADHD and his therapist strongly advised a trial with a medication. "I can focus, but I can't pee or sleep." He was started on Strattera 25 mg a day week 1, 40 mg a day week 2, and last week increased to 60 mg daily. He reports that over a week ago he started having difficulty urinating, trouble sleeping, no appetite and "I feel like my heart is racing out of my chest." He states his symptoms of ADHD have improved greatly, but feels that the side effects are not worth it.

Family History: Brother and sister treated for ADHD, Dad treated for depression

Medical History: Broken shoulder from skiing accident

Substance Use: 3-4 caffeinated sodas daily   Medications: Paxil CR 25 mg

What do you do?

Any idea what happened? The symptoms of ADHD have been treated well with Strattera, but the side effects are potentially dangerous.

Options

1. Decrease or discontinue Strattera

Strattera has worked for David's ADHD, but the side effects are intolerable. Lowering the dose may continue to treat his symptoms and reduce the side effects.

2. Psychostimulants

Medications used in the treatment of ADHD include methylphenidate (Ritalin, Concerta, Metadate, Focalin), mixed salts of a single-entity amphetamine product (Adderall, Adderall XR, Vyvanse), and dextroamphetamine (Dexedrine, Dextrostat). They are available as both short- and long-acting preparations. Methamphetamine (Desoxyn) is rarely used for ADHD, but is another option.

3. Off-label use of Provigil

Provigil (modafinil) has demonstrated efficacy in treating ADHD yet it has been approved by the FDA only to treat excessive sleepiness due to obstructive sleep apnea, shift work sleep disorder and narcolepsy. A careful sleep history is always important to rule out co-existing problems such as sleep apnea.

My Choice

David is having a drug interaction. Strattera is primarily eliminated through the cytochrome P450 2D6 pathway (CYP2D6). Paxil CR inhibits or slows down the elimination of Strattera in this pathway. This causes higher plasma concentration levels of Strattera and results in increased risk of side effects even with normal doses. In addition, David may be a poor metabolizer of the 2D6 drugs and can have the same response to medications eliminated in the 2D6 pathway even without the presence of other drugs. It is important to get a full medication history before starting anything new.

First things first! Lower the dose of Strattera to 10 mg and check his response and side effects.

Medications are not the only things that can interact with other drugs. Grapefruit juice can interfere with drug metabolism. Nicotine and caffeine are also culprits for changing the way some medications are metabolized.

AmpliChip CYP450 is an FDA-approved test that analyzes blood DNA to detect genetic variations in how patients metabolize medications. It specifically looks at cytochrome P450 2D6 and 2C19 enzymes. The test is currently being marketed to the psychiatric community but it is often difficult to get insurance to cover it.

Likely side effects

Strattera can cause constipation, dry mouth, nausea, decreased appetite, problems sleeping, sexual problems.

Risks

David's problem with urination may not resolve with lower levels of Strattera, and he may develop high blood pressure.

Drug Interactions

P450 Family	Inhibitors	Inducers	Substrates	
			Psychiatric	**Non-psychiatric**
3A4	**Prozac Luvox Serzone Grapefruit juice**	**Tegretol St. John's Wort** Less significant: **Trileptal Topamax Provigil**	**Buspar** (Inh: N/V, dizziness, sedation) **Tricyclics** (Inh: sedation, arrhythmias) **Xanax** (Inh: sedation) **Methadone** (Inh: sedation, miosis; Ind: opioid withdrawal) **Tegretol** (Inh: fatigue, confusion; Ind: seizures) **Risperdal, Seroquel, Abilify** (Ind: breakthrough psychosis)	**Calcium Channel Blockers** (Inh: hypotension) **Birth Control Pills** (Ind: pregnancy) **Statins,** except Pravachol (Inh: elevated LFTs. rhabdomyolysis) **Cyclosporine** (Ind: transplant rejection)
2D6	**Prozac Paxil Zoloft** (>150mg/d) **Wellbutrin Tricyclics**	No inducers	**Tricyclics Effexor Abilify Cymbalta**	**Beta-Blockers** (Inh: hypotension) **Vicodin** (Inh: pro-drug—less analgesia) **Tramadol/Ultram** (Inh: pro-drug—less analgesia)
1A2	**Luvox**	**Cigarettes**	**Clozapine** (Inh: orthostasis, sedation) **Zyprexa** (Inh: sedation, constipation; Ind: decompensation) **Caffeine** (Inh: jittery) **Rozerem, Cymbalta**	None of great significance
2C9/2C19	**Luvox Prozac Depakote** (2C9 only)	No significant psychiatric inducers	None of great significance	**Oral Hypoglycemics** (2C9-Inh: low blood sugar) **Dilantin**
Protein Binding	**Prozac Paxil Zoloft Depakote**	N/A	None of great significance	**Coumadin** (Inh: elevated PT, bruising, bleeding) **Digoxin** (Inh: arrhythmia, N/V, confusion) **Dilantin** (Inh: confusion, ataxia)
Miscellaneous	Depakote and Zoloft increase levels of Lamictal Luvox increases levels of Haldol and Rozerem			

Key: "Inh" = inhibition; "Ind" = induction; "N/V" = nausea/vomiting; "pro-drug" means that parent compound is metabolized into the active agent; in these cases, inhibition leads to less drug activity.

Adapted from The Carlat Report on Psychiatric Treatment (www.TheCarlatReport.com), 2003, Volume 1 number 7.
Copyright © Clearview Publishing 2003. Used with permission.

Resources

Web Sites

Drug Interactions Cytochrome P450 System
www.medicine.iupui.edu/flockhart

P450, UGT, and P-gp Drug Interactions
www.mhc.com/Cytochromes

Medscape Drug Interaction Checker
www.medscape.com/druginfo/druginterchecker

Drug Information Online
www.drugs.com/drug_interactions.html

Center for Drug Evaluation and Research
www.fda.gov/cder/drug/drugsafety/drugindex.htm

Books

Drug Interactions Casebook: The Cytochrome P450 System and Beyond
Neil Sandson et al.
American Psychiatric Publishing, 2003

The Top 100 Drug Interactions: A Guide to Patient Management
Philip D. Hansten and John Horn
H & H Publications, 2008

A-Z Guide to Drug-Herb-Vitamin Interactions Revised and Expanded 2nd Edition: Improve Your Health and Avoid Side Effects When Using Common Medications and Natural Supplements Together
Alan R. Gaby
Three Rivers Press, 2006

Drug Metabolism in Psychiatry: A Clinical Guide
David Carlat
Clearview Publishing, 2006

Case of

Ned NoMeds

Ned NoMeds, a 12-year-old male, is brought in by his mother because he is refusing to take his Ritalin (methylphenidate). He was first diagnosed with ADHD in second grade by his pediatrician, who has followed him since. After Ned started taking Ritalin, his academic performance markedly improved and he was much easier to manage at home. At Parkview Elementary the school nurse was able to dispense his medications during the mid-morning recess. This fall, however, he started attending Riverview Middle School and refused to visit the nurse's office for fear of ridicule by his friends. Ned will take his morning Ritalin before leaving home and does well for the first two periods of school. However, his grades in his afternoon algebra and chemistry classes are poor. His soccer coach wonders why his on-field performance has deteriorated this year. Mom notes that he picks more fights and has trouble completing homework in the evening.

Family History: Older brother has ADHD.

Medical History: None   Substance Use: Denies

Medications: Ritalin 15 mg three times daily (only takes in AM, however)

What do you do?

Ned presents a clinical challenge: treating adolescents with ADHD. He clearly benefits from treatment but is asserting his independence by refusing to take meds at school. Luckily, there are several approaches available.

Diagnosis: Attention Deficit Hyperactivity Disorder (ADHD)

Options

1. No medications—psychotherapy alone

ADHD research has shown that children treated with both psychotherapy and medication show more improvement than those who were treated with either alone. Parents in the studies are also happier with a combination strategy.

The most effective psychotherapy for these children is behavior therapy. Interventions focus on modifying the environment to change the child's behavior. We must remember that 20% of children with ADHD do not respond to currently available medication.

2. Treat with long-acting methylphenidate

One of the biggest problems with Ritalin is that it lasts only three to four hours. Luckily, there are now many long-acting preparations available that have the same active ingredient—methylphenidate. Concerta, Ritalin LA (long acting, not Los Angeles), Metadate CD (controlled delivery), Focalin XR, and Methylin (chewable and oral solution). These are all taken orally but there is also a patch called Daytrana that kids wear on their hip for 9 hours at a time.

3. Treat with an amphetamine

Adderall (D, L amphetamine), Adderall XR, Vyvanse, Dexedrine, Dexedrine Spansule, and Dextrostat (D-amphetamine) are also stimulant medications approved to treat ADHD. If methylphenidate is not tolerated or ineffective, these meds are another option.

4. Treat with a non-stimulant

Strattera (atomoxetine) was approved by the FDA in 2003. It takes considerably longer to work than the stimulants and generally is seen as less effective. For children who cannot tolerate stimulants, it is an alternative. Be careful of using Strattera if there is a family history of bipolar disorder. We have seen manic activation in some patients.

My Choice

Treating children with ADHD requires knowledge of their daily schedule: When do they start and end school? At what times are their most challenging subjects? What are their extracurricular activities and when? Then one tailors their treatment to their routine. Stimulants are the most effective treatment for ADHD; we start with this medicine class unless there is a good reason not to.

In Ned's case, we know that methylphenidate works. He needs a longer acting preparation to carry him throughout his day. Concerta mimics three times daily Ritalin and is the best option for Ned. We would start him on 36 mg each morning and titrate up to 2 mg/kg/day if necessary. A daily Daytrana patch would also be an option.

Likely side effects

All stimulants can contribute to loss of appetite. We avoid this by having children eat before taking their meds. We encourage parents to give frequent high quality, high calorie snacks such as protein shakes and energy bars. Remember that appetite returns when the stimulants wear off, so be prepared for hungry children at bedtime. Medication patches can cause skin irritation.

Stimulants can also make falling asleep more difficult. This can be avoided by choosing the proper formulation. Recent research supporting the use of melatonin for insomnia in ADHD children is encouraging.

Risks

Growth delay is a concern with these children. It now appears that ADHD children are smaller than their non-ADHD peers (even if not on medication) but they catch up in adolescence. Still, it is important to monitor height and weight and educate the family about proper nutrition.

Resources

Web Sites

Helpful fact sheets
www.addwarehouse.com
www.chadd.org

The Carlat Report, Volume 4 Number 9
www.thecarlatreport.com/index.asp?page=wp3162007141052
This is an excellent review of the treatment options.

Books

Straight Talk about Psychiatric Medications for Kids (3rd edition)
Timothy Wilens
Guilford Press, 2008

The ADHD Book of Lists: A Practical Guide for Helping Children and Teens with Attention Deficit Disorders
Sandra Rief
Jossey-Bass, 2003

Landmark Research

MTA Study
Arch Gen Psychiatry 1999; 56:1073-1086.
Multimodal treatment study of children with
ADHD

This is the largest placebo-controlled trial of ADHD treatments. It compares stimulants, behavioral treatments and combined strategies.

Practice Guidelines

Practice Parameter for the Assessment and Treatment of Children and Adolescents with A-D/HD in *JAACAP* (2007) 46 (7) 894-921.

ADHD Drugs

Medication	Dose	Available Doses	Duration of Action	Generic Available?	Notes
Methylphenidates					
Short acting					
Ritalin	5-30mg BID	10, 20	3-4 hrs	Yes	
Focalin	2.5-10mg BID	2.5, 5, 10	3-4 hrs	No	D-isomer of Ritalin
Methylin	5-30mg BID	5, 10, 20	3-4 hrs	"branded generic" of Ritalin	
Methylin CT	5-30mg BID	2.5, 5, 10	3-4 hrs	No	Chewable
Methylin Oral Solution	5-30mg BID	5mg/5ml, 10mg/5ml	3-4 hrs	No	Clear, grape-flavored liquid
Intermediate acting					
Ritalin SR	20-60mg q AM	20	4-8 hrs	Yes	Continuous release (less predictable because of wax matrix)
Metadate ER	20-60mg q AM	10, 20	4-8 hrs	"branded generic" of Ritalin SR	Continuous release (less predictable because of wax matrix)
Methylin ER	20-60mg q AM	10, 20	4-8 hrs	"branded generic" of Ritalin SR	Hydrophilic polymer, so possibly more continuous than others in category
Long acting					
Concerta	18-72mg q AM	18, 27, 36, 54	12 hrs	No	Initial bolus, then continuous
Metadate CD	20-60mg q AM	10, 20, 30	8 hrs	No	Mimics BID dosing; beads Can be sprinkled
Focalin XR	5-30mg qD	5, 10, 20	8 hrs	No	
Ritalin LA	20-60mg q AM	20, 30, 40	8-12 hrs	No	Mimics BID dosing; beads Can be sprinkled
Daytrana	10-30mg qD	10, 15, 20, 30	8-12 hrs	No	Continuous release patch, duration can be shortened by decreasing wear time

Medication	Dose	Available Doses	Duration of Action	Generic Available?	Notes
Amphetamines					
Short acting					
Dexedrine	5-20mg BID	5	3-5 hrs	Yes	Dextroamphetamine
Dextrostat	5-20mg BID	5, 10	3-5 hrs	"branded generic" of Dexedrine	Dextroamphetamine
Desoxyn	5-10mg BID	5	3-5 hrs	Yes	Methamphetamine
Intermediate acting					
Adderall	5-30mg BID or 5-60mg q AM	5, 10, 20, 30	4-8 hrs	Yes	Mixed salt of l- and d-amphetamine
Long acting					
Dexedrine Spansules	20mg q AM	5, 10, 15	8-12 hrs	Yes	Initial bolus, then continuous; beads
Adderall XR	5-30mg q AM	5, 10, 15, 20, 25, 30	8-12 hrs	Yes	Mixed salt of l- and d-amphetamine; beads; mimics BID dosing
Vyvanse	20-70mg q AM	20, 30, 40, 50, 60, 70	8-12 hrs	No	Inactive "pro-drug" which has no pharmacologic effect until after it is absorbed through the GI tract
Non-stimulant					
Strattera	0.5mg/kg 1-2 mg/kg	10, 18, 25, 40, 60	24 hrs	No	atomoxetine

Case of

Hyper Harry

Hyper Harry is an 8-year-old boy referred by his pediatrician, who has been treating him for ADHD since he was in kindergarten. Since starting Ritalin (methylphenidate), Harry has had difficulty falling asleep. Harry's mother states that although he is ready for bed at 9 p.m., he is usually up and about until midnight or later. He states that he is unable to fall asleep despite being quite active all day.

Previous trials of Adderall, Concerta and Dexedrine also contributed to insomnia and appetite suppression. When Harry is off medication, he spends his school days in the principal's office because he is unable to tolerate the stimulation of his class.

Family History: Harry's father has ADHD but does not take medication.

Medical History: None   Substance Use: Denies

Medications: Ritalin 10 mg twice daily

What do you do?

Harry clearly meets the criteria for ADHD but has problems with stimulant side effects. Luckily, there are several treatment options. Any child with ADHD and insomnia also needs to be evaluated for a sleep disorder such as Restless Legs Syndrome or Obstructive Sleep Apnea Syndrome.

Diagnosis: Attention Deficit Hyperactivity Disorder (ADHD)

Options

1. No medications—psychotherapy alone

Harry has been in individual treatment since he was six years old. While it has helped him to understand his disorder and improve his behavior, psychotherapy alone is not effective for Harry.

2. Treat with long-acting methylphenidate

Concerta, Ritalin LA, Metadate CD, and Focalin XR are long-acting medications using the same active ingredient—methylphenidate. Recent studies suggest that appetite suppression and insomnia may be less of a problem with Focalin XR than the others. Focalin is the d-isomer of methylphenidate and requires half the dose.

3. Treat with an amphetamine

Harry had significant side effects with Adderall and Dexedrine in the past. It is unlikely that this class of medication will be successfully tolerated.

4. Treat with a non-stimulant

Strattera (atomoxetine) is a norepinephrine reuptake inhibitor that is not a stimulant. It takes time to build up a sufficient dosage. There is a risk of liver problems with Strattera that could require monitoring with blood tests.

5. Continue Ritalin; try other agents to increase weight and sleep

Many augmentation strategies have been used to try to minimize stimulant side effects. Remeron (mirtazapine) is an antidepressant with the potential of sedation and weight gain as side effects. Recent research suggests that melatonin may be helpful for sleep onset in ADHD children. One downside of this strategy is the use of medications that are not approved by the FDA for pediatric populations.

My Choice

Harry's academic and social life suffers when he is not taking his medications, but his current regimen is contributing to weight loss and insomnia. We need to keep trying available options until we find one that is effective and tolerable.

Since methylphenidate products have been effective for Harry, we would switch to Focalin XR. which may cause fewer problems and may be effective for as long as twelve hours. To counteract any appetite suppression that may occur, it is important to instruct the parents to feed Harry healthy, high-calorie meals before he takes his morning meds and in the evening when the medication is leaving his system. The equivalent dose of Ritalin 10 mg BID would be Focalin XR 10 mg qAM.

We would certainly continue Harry's therapy.

Likely side effects

Always watch for appetite suppression and insomnia with ADHD medications.

Risks

We would continue to monitor Harry's height and weight on Focalin XR. Need to check an EKG if he has any cardiac complaints.

Resources

Web Sites

National Sleep Foundation's site for children
www.sleepforkids.org

www.sleepfoundation.org
Children and sleep

Books

Healthy Sleep Habits, Happy Child
Marc Weissbluth
Ballantine Books, 2005

Sleep Better! A Guide to Improving Sleep for Children With Special Needs
Vincent Mark Durand
Brookes Publishing, 1997

ADHD & Me: What I Learned from Lighting Fires at the Dinner Table
Blake E.S. Taylor
New Harbinger Publications 2008

Papers

Christopher J Kratochvil, MD et al. Pharmacological Management of
Treatment-Induced Insomnia in ADHD
Journal of the American Academy of Child & Adolescent Psychiatry.
44(5):499-501, May 2005

Practice Guidelines

Pharmacologic Management of Insomnia in Children and Adolescents:
Consensus Statement
Jodi A. Mindell, PhD et al
PEDIATRICS Vol. 117 No. 6 June 2006, pp. e1223-e1232

Case of

Restless Rita

Rita, a 33-year-old divorced female, presents after seeing a television ad for Strattera, wondering if she has adult attention deficit disorder.

She complains of a lifelong history of inattention and impulsivity. Her academic and employment histories are erratic. She did not graduate from college and has never held a job longer than one year.

Family History: Eight-year-old son takes Concerta for ADHD. Mother has taken antidepressants in the past.

Medical History: Anemia

Substance Use: 4 coffees + 3 Diet Cokes daily abused alcohol in college—now drinks rarely

Medications: Iron supplements

What do you do?

It is becoming increasingly common for adults to present for treatment wondering whether they have ADHD. We often end up evaluating the parents after their children have been referred by school personnel.

Rita has classic adult ADHD symptoms with social, vocational and academic consequences and could likely benefit from medication. The use of a rating scale designed for adult ADHD would help us to accurately list the pattern and degree of symptoms for diagnostic purposes and to help guide future treatment decisions.

Diagnosis: Attention Deficit Hyperactivity Disorder (ADHD)

Options

1. No medications—psychotherapy alone

Psychotherapy alone for adults with ADHD is often ineffective. However, there is a place for life coaching skills to help manage academic and vocational situations. Rating scales and neuropsychiatric testing may help to quantify Rita's impairment.

2. Treat with stimulants

There are many choices for ADHD. The first decision is whether or not to use a stimulant such as Ritalin or Adderall. Stimulants are clearly the most effective meds for ADHD, but not everyone can tolerate the side effects that can include decreased appetite (young women rarely complain about *this* problem), insomnia and tremor. In our experience, most young adults do very well on stimulant medications.

3. Treat with non-stimulant Strattera

Another FDA-approved option is Strattera (atomoxetine). We see disruptive side effects with Strattera including sedation and urinary retention. Another possibility is manic activation. Fortunately, Strattera is not a controlled substance and is unlikely to be abused. Also, Strattera provides around-the-clock coverage, which can be important if Rita experiences early morning disorganization.

4. Use a non-FDA approved medication

Alternatives that are not approved by the FDA for adult ADHD include Provigil (modafinil) and Wellbutrin (bupropion). Generally these are reserved for patients who cannot tolerate stimulants or Strattera.

My Choice

Adderall XR. Although there are many stimulants on the market today, most are short acting and need to be taken throughout the day and early evening. We prefer medication strategies that are simple and easy to remember (especially for patients who have difficulties with organizational skills). Adults usually begin Adderall XR 20 mg each morning. Dose is increased by 5-10 mg daily each week until symptoms are controlled. Maximum dose is 60 mg/day. Concerta is another long-acting option. If her son has done well on Concerta, this might be the best (and simplest) choice.

Likely side effects

Adderall/Concerta: Decreased appetite, rapid heartbeat, increased blood pressure.

Risks

Sudden death, stroke, and myocardial infarction have been reported in adults taking stimulant drugs at the usual doses for ADHD. It is important to take any cardiac symptom seriously.

Stimulants can be abused. We would hesitate giving Adderall or Concerta in a patient with a history of significant drug abuse. Rita has a distant history of alcohol abuse and would need to be cautioned about the abuse potential. Vyvanse is a pro-drug that requires activation in the gut – as a result you can not get high by snorting or using it IV. Of course, you may be able to get high by taking it orally!

Resources

Web Sites

Attention Deficit Disorder Association
www.addvance.com
www.add.org/articles/women.html

The Center: A resource for women and girls with AD/HD
www.ncgiadd.org

Gender Issues in ADHD
www.apa.org/monitor/feb03/adhd.html

Books

Survival Tips for Women with AD/HD: Beyond Piles, Palms and Post-its
Terry Matlen
Specialty Press/A.D.D. Warehouse, 2005

Delivered from Distraction: Getting the Most out of Life with Attention Deficit Disorder
Ed Hallowell and John Ratey
Ballantine Books, 2005

Women with Attention Deficit Disorder: Embrace Your Differences and Transform Your Life
Sari Solden
Underwood Books, 2005

You Mean I'm Not Lazy, Stupid or Crazy?!: The Classic Self-Help Book for Adults with Attention Deficit Disorder
Kate Kelly et al.
Scriber, 2006

ADD-Friendly Ways to Organize Your Life
Judith Kolberg and Kathleen Nadeau
Routledge, 2002

Case of

Tom Sawyer's Twin

Tom, a 9-year-old male, is referred by his elementary school counselor for medication. He is in fourth grade, and IQ tests put Tom in the highly gifted category. Teachers have had a difficult time challenging Tom in the classroom. He has strong feelings about right and wrong, is quick to disagree with authority figures and sometimes refuses to do homework "because it is inane." His grades range from A's to D's depending on the subject. Tom's parents have difficulty disciplining him; he speaks passionately about life not being fair when asked to help around the house. He is actively involved in tennis, swim team, and chess club. He has several good friends that share his passions.

Family History: None

Medical History: None   Substance Use: Denies

Medications: Claritin for seasonal allergies

What do you do?

Tom is a very intelligent boy with much on his mind. A thorough diagnostic examination reveals no learning disorders. Rating scales from his teachers vary wildly. Some find him annoying; others see no problems at all.

Diagnosis: None

Options

1. No medications—psychotherapy alone

Highly gifted children have special academic and emotional needs. Tom is not adequately challenged in his current school, and alternate educational options need to be considered. These children often succeed in specialized classrooms geared towards all of the needs of highly able students.

Family therapy can be extremely helpful for the parents to learn new coping strategies.

2. Treat with stimulants

Some of Tom's teachers say that he is unfocused and distractible. If this were a consistent finding, a diagnosis of ADHD needs to be explored. A commonly heard myth is that you can tell if someone has ADHD by his or her response to stimulants. This

38

is clearly untrue. Almost everyone is able to concentrate better on a low dose of a stimulant. Why do you think coffee is so popular?

3. Treat with Strattera (atomoxetine)

A popular approach has become to treat ADHD with a non-stimulant medication such as Strattera. Stimulants are highly regulated (called Schedule II) by the DEA and require monthly, handwritten prescriptions on special pads. Because Strattera is not a scheduled drug, a prescription can be telephoned to the pharmacy with refills.

There are a few short term head-to-head studies comparing stimulants directly to Strattera, and the overall consensus among psychiatrists is that stimulants work much better for most children. If stimulants fail or cause significant side effects or if the patient and parents do not want a scheduled drug, Strattera is a reasonable choice.

4. Treat with an antidepressant

Tom's occasional oppositional behavior could be a symptom of a mood disorder. There is no evidence of this from our interview with Tom and his parents.

My Choice

Tom needs a different placement in school. We have seen remarkable "psychiatric" improvement when children are matched with the appropriate teacher and classroom. A thorough educational evaluation will help to determine the proper learning environment.

Dr. Lawrence Diller, a California behavior pediatrician recently describes similar children in an interview published in The Carlat Report (April 2005):

"ADHD is for the kids who are definitely struggling in school, have some problems with impulse control, have interests and talents that are not necessarily what the adults want, but when these kids are interested in something, they focus fine. That kind of behavior has been redefined as pathology, and there is no question in my mind that Tom Sawyer and Huck Finn would be taking medications today."

Likely side effects

No medicine—no side effects

Risks

If Tom does in fact have ADHD and is not treated, his risk for developing a substance abuse disorder is significantly increased.

Resources

Web Sites

www.hoagiesgifted.org
A comprehensive resource for parents and educators of gifted children.

www.sengifted.org
Supporting the emotional needs of gifted children

The Carlat Report
www.thecarlatreport.com
Volume 3 Number 4
Treating ADHD; contains the interview with Dr. Diller

Books

Running on Ritalin: A Physician Reflects on Children, Society and Performance in a Pill
Lawrence Diller
Bantam Books, 1999

Should I Medicate My Child? Sane Solutions for Troubled Kids—With and without Psychiatric Drugs
Lawrence Diller
Basic Books, 2008

Should You Medicate Your Child's Mind? :A Child Psychiatrist Makes Sense of Whether or Not to Give Kids Meds
Elizabeth Roberts
Da Capo, 2006

Genius Denied: How to Stop Wasting our Brightest Young Minds
Jan Davidson
Simon and Schuster, 2005

Misdiagnosis and Dual Diagnoses of Gifted Children and Adults
James T. Webb
Great Potential Press, 2005

Cognitive Disorders

Case of
Forgetful Fabian

Fabian, a 78-year-old married male, presents with his wife because he is becoming increasingly forgetful. Over the last several years Fabian has been losing his car keys, his wallet, and his checkbook. He accuses their cleaning lady of 15 years of stealing his glasses and his medications. Last week, he went for a walk and could not remember how to return to his home.

Family History: Mother died at 94 in a nursing home. Father died at age 55 of heart problems.

Medical History: Hypertension   Substance Use: None

Medications: Hydrochlorothiazide

What do you do?

Fabian appears to have a slowly progressing dementing illness. It is important to consider other reasons for cognitive decline such as depression, medications, low thyroid, brain tumors, the list goes on and on. Up to 15% of dementias have reversible factors. Fabian's comprehensive medical and psychiatric workup is negative.

Diagnosis: Dementia, Alzheimer's type

Options

1. No medications

Referrals need to be made so that Fabian's wife can continue to function as his caregiver. The local Alzheimer's Association has abundant resources. Adult day-care and home health are options. Investigate your state's Division of Aging as this government agency has access to other local and state agencies. Refer Fabian's family to an experienced lawyer or financial planner to ensure that estate planning is adequate.

2. Treat with antipsychotics

Paranoia is a common symptom of advancing dementia. As Fabian loses his cognitive capacity, he looks to blame others for his mistakes. Antipsychotics may be helpful if he becomes agitated or difficult to control. The atypical agents generally are much better tolerated in the elderly than older agents such as Haldol (haloperidol). However, the FDA has issued a public health advisory warning healthcare providers, patients, and patient caregivers against the off-label use of atypical antipsychotic medications for the treatment of dementia-related behavior disorders in the elderly due to an increased risk of mortality.

3. Treat with Aricept (donepezil)—a cholinesterase inhibitor

Aricept inhibits one enzyme that inactivates acetylcholine. By inhibiting this destruction, the neurotransmitter acetylcholine increases—which should help with Fabian's symptoms.

4. Treat with Razadyne (galantamine)

Razadyne also inhibits this enzyme, but it also works on nicotine receptors. This causes brain cells to release more acetylcholine, which again is associated with improved cognition.

5. Treat with Exelon (rivastigmine)

Exelon inhibits both enzymes that inactivate acetylcholine. In theory, this should make it more effective.

6. Treat with Namenda (memantine)

Namenda attaches to the N-Methyl-D-Aspartade (NMDA) receptors in the brain, which helps to regulate the activity of glutamate. The right amount of glutamate is necessary for the brain to process information—this may be disturbed in dementia.

My Choice

Social support is crucial if Fabian is to remain at home with his family. We would discuss medication treatment with Fabian and his wife. Combining Namenda with Aricept or Reminyl covers both the acetylcholine and glutamate bases. It is very important to understand that these medications usually do not restore a patient back to their baseline level of functioning. Instead we hope to decrease the risk of further cognitive decline.

Exelon is associated with a high rate of nausea and vomiting and can be very difficult to tolerate.

Likely side effects

GI upset, dizziness on cholinesterase inhibitors; dizziness and headache with Namenda

Risks

Studies show that if a patient stops Aricept, even temporarily, cognitive functioning can worsen dramatically.

Resources

Web Sites

Alzheimer's Association
www.alz.org

Alzheimer's Disease Education and Referral Center, a service of the National Institute on Aging
www.nia.nih.gov/alzheimers

Books

The 36-Hour Day: A Family Guide to Caring for Persons With Alzheimer Disease, Related Dementing Illnesses, and Memory Loss in Later Life
Nancy L. Mace and Peter V. Rabins
Johns Hopkins University Press, 2006
A classic, now fourth edition. Very helpful to caregivers.

Courage to Care: A Caregiver's Guide Through Each Stage of Alzheimer's
Joanne Parrent
Alpha, 2001

Alzheimer's Early Stages: First Steps for Family, Friends, and Caregivers
Daniel Kuhn
Hunter House, 2003

The Alzheimer's Action Plan: The Experts' Guide to the Best Diagnosis and Treatment for Memory Problems
P. Murali Doraiswamy, Lisa P. Gwyther, Tina Adler
St Martin's Press, 2008

APA practice guidelines

Treating Alzheimer's Disease and Other Dementias of Late Life, Second Edition
www.psychiatryonline.com/pracGuide/pracGuideTopic_3.aspx

Medical Letter

Atypical Antipsychotics in the Elderly
Volume 47 (Issue 1214)
August 1, 2005

FORGETFUL FABIAN

Medications to Treat Alzheimer's			
Drug name	**Drug type and treatment**	**Manufacturer's recommended dosage**	**Common side effects**
Namenda (memantine) Blocks the toxic effects associated with excess glutamate and regulates glutamate activation	N-methyl D-aspartate (NMDA) antagonist prescribed to treat symptoms of moderate to severe Alzheimer's	5mg, once a day Increase to 10mg/day (5mg twice a day), 15mg/day (5mg and 10mg as separate doses), and 20mg/day (10mg twice a day) at a minimum of 1 week intervals if well tolerated	Dizziness, headache, constipation, confusion
Razadyne (formerly known as Reminyl) (galantamine) Prevents the breakdown of acetylcholine and stimulates nicotinic receptors to release more acetylcholine in the brain	Cholinesterase inhibitor prescribed to treat symptoms of mild to moderate Alzheimer's	4mg, twice a day (8mg/day) Increase by 8mg/day after 4 weeks to 8mg, twice a day	Nausea, vomiting, diarrhea, weight loss
Exelon (rivastigmine) Prevents the breakdown of acetylcholine and butyrylcholine (a brain chemical similar to acetylcholine) in the brain	Cholinesterase inhibitor prescribed to treat symptoms of mild to moderate Alzheimer's	1.5mg, twice a day (3mg/day) Increase by 3mg/day every 2 weeks to 6mg, twice a day (12mg/day) if well tolerated	Nausea, vomiting, weight loss, upset stomach, muscle weakness
Aricept (donepezil) Prevents the breakdown of acetylcholine in the brain	Cholinesterase inhibitor prescribed to treat symptoms of mild to moderate Alzheimer's	5mg, once a day Increase after 4-6 weeks to 10mg, once a day if well tolerated	Nausea, diarrhea, vomiting
Cognex (tacrine) Prevents the breakdown of acetylcholine in the brain Note: Cognex is still available, but no longer actively marketed by the manufacturer	Cholinesterase inhibitor prescribed to treat symptoms of mild to moderate Alzheimer's	10mg, four times a day (40mg/day) Increase by 40mg/day every 4 weeks to 40mg, four times a day (160mg/day), if liver enzyme functions remain normal and if well tolerated	Nausea, diarrhea, possible liver damage

Adapted from www.alz.org/ Alzheimer's Association

Eating Disorders

Case of

Anorexic Angela

A 12-year-old girl is referred by her mother. Since Angela started middle school, her weight has been steadily decreasing. Angela attributes this to her vegetarian diet. Her mother reports that six months ago her daughter decided to become vegetarian. Eight weeks ago, she turned vegan and further restricted what she was "allowed" to eat. Worried about her health, Angela was sent to her pediatrician who discovered that she had lost 15 pounds in the last four months.

Angela says that she doesn't want to be "one of those fat girls who wear tight jeans." She will only eat lettuce, brown rice and popcorn. She thinks her doctor's scale is inaccurate and that she actually is a bit chubbier than last year.

Angela's grades are excellent and she is on the gymnastics and track teams at school. Her mother reports that Angela has always been a perfectionist.

Family History: Mother has struggled with being overweight since her own adolescence.

Medical History: Negative. Angela is 5 feet 2 inches tall and weighs 80 pounds.

Medications: None

What do you do?

Angela exhibits classical warning signs of girls with anorexia nervosa. A vegetarian diet may be selected by the child to camouflage a pre-existing eating disorder. She is at the 25th percentile for height and much below the 3rd percentile for weight. If she continues to lose weight, it becomes a medical emergency. Eating disorders begin in adolescence a whopping 85% of the time.

Diagnosis: Anorexia nervosa, restricting type

Options

1. No medications—psychotherapy only

Eating disorders can be treated with many approaches—family therapy (to help support and educate family members and to explore interpersonal interactions that may feed the problem), individual counseling (in part to help recognize flawed thoughts about body image and self esteem), and group therapy with other eating disorder patients. Investigation must be made into the possibility of precipitating abuse or trauma.

2. No medications—nutritional counseling only

Medical nutrition therapy is an important part of the treatment of anorexics but is not sufficient alone.

3. Try an antidepressant

Depressive symptoms are not uncommon in anorexics. It would make sense to use a medicine that is likely to cause increased appetite, but it is unclear whether it would provide any additional benefit. We find anorexic girls to be very sensitive to sedating side effects, so although Remeron may increase appetite, we do not find it acceptable to most of our adolescents. SSRIs have been the most commonly used antidepressants—Prozac (fluoxetine) and Zoloft (sertraline) leading the way. Serotonergic antidepressants may also treat the obsessional thinking that accompanies eating disorders. We would, however, avoid Anafranil (clomipramine) due to its potential cardiac risks. Luvox (fluvoxamine) is approved for OCD and social anxiety disorders, and sometimes can be of help in patients like Angela.

4. Treat with an atypical antipsychotic

People's thinking about their weight and body image borders on psychotic when they seem to have lost touch with reality. Many of these drugs are associated with increased appetite: Zyprexa (olanzapine) especially. Zyprexa may help reduce anxiety and decrease rigid and obsessional thinking. Generally, low doses are sufficient.

My Choice

Do not try to treat Angela by yourself! The care of eating disordered girls must be provided by an interdisciplinary team consisting of a minimum of a pediatrician or family physician, psychiatrist, therapist and nutritionist. We also strongly recommend a dental exam, although this a greater concern in bulimics. Anorexic patients are notoriously resistant to treatment, and a collaborative effort provides the best chance of recovery. Attention to medical complications is important.

I would try Angela on a serotonergic agent such as Luvox. Always start at a low dose on these underweight girls. This medication can be sedating. Start at 25 mg at bedtime and gradually increase to as much as 150 mg. (Luvox CR is not approved in children) Another SSRI such as Prozac might be more activating. Zyprexa is another reasonable strategy. Start at 2.5 mg QHS and gradually increase to 10 mg if necessary.

Likely side effects, risks

Luvox: Sedation, nausea initially, and possible drug interactions. Although it is not approved for depression by the FDA, Luvox is an antidepressant. The usual precautions for suicidal or homicidal activation must be in place.

Zyprexa: Sedation, increased appetite, possibility of increasing blood levels of lipids and glucose.

Resources

Web Sites

Face the Issue www.facetheissue.com

Something Fishy www.something-fishy.org

National Eating Disorders Association www.nationaleatingdisorders.org

Anorexia Nervosa and Associated Disorders www.anad.org

Books

Help Your Teenager Beat an Eating Disorder
James Lock and Daniel LeGrange
Guilford Press, 2005

Nourishing Your Daughter: Help your child develop a healthy relationship with food and her body
Carol Beck
Perigee Books, 2001

Stick Figure: A Diary of My Former Self
Lori Gottlieb
Berkley Publishing Group, 2001

Surviving Ophelia: Mothers Share Their Wisdom in Navigating the Tumultuous Teenage Years
Cheryl Dellasega
Ballantine Books, 2002

Practice Guidelines

American Psychiatric Association
Practice Guideline for the Treatment of Patients with Eating Disorders, Third Edition
http://www.psychiatryonline.com/pracGuide/pracGuideChapToc_12.aspx

---

Mood Disorders

Case of
Amelia Airheart

Amelia, a 30-year-old single female math teacher, presents with depressive and anxiety symptoms.

Amelia, a licensed pilot since age 16, has been tearful, mildly anxious, and sad for the last three months. She denies suicidal ideation and continues to function well socially and at her job.

Family History: Mother takes an unknown antidepressant for "nerves."

Medical History: Migraines   Substance Use: Occasional alcohol

Medications: Multivitamins and calcium

What do you do?

A thorough physical examination must be completed because there may be comorbid medical conditions complicating her depression. Although Amelia meets the criteria for major depressive disorder, she is still functioning well. If she takes a prescription antidepressant, she will not be allowed to fly per FAA regulations.

Diagnosis: Major depression, single episode

Options

1. No medications—refer for psychotherapy

Cognitive Behavior Therapy (CBT) has been shown to be quite effective in mild to moderate cases of depression.

2. Treat with natural supplement

St. John's wort, SAM-e, and Omega 3 Fatty Acids have been shown in some clinical trials to be effective for depression.

3. Treat with an SSRI

SSRIs such as Prozac (fluoxetine), Zoloft (sertraline) and Lexapro (escitalopram) are very helpful for mild to moderate depressive episodes. However, she will be forced to give up her pilot's license if she takes a prescription medication for depression.

My Choice

Amelia is a great candidate for cognitive behavior psychotherapy. She is well-educated and highly motivated. We would also recommend that she investigate natural treatments because prescription antidepressants would create a significant stressor—loss of her pilot's license. Omega 3 fatty acids are proven to be helpful in preventing heart attacks and may favorably impact mood. It is important to take the EPA component and to use at least 1 gram daily. SAM-e has been shown in many studies to be effective in depression with minimal side effects. Doses of up to 1600 mg/day may be needed. St. John's wort is better known but has many drug interactions that can be problematic. Of course, any treatment needs to be approved by Amelia's Aviation Medical Examiner. Pilots should not fly when they are depressed!

Likely side effects

Omega 3 fatty acids: Nausea, diarrhea and a fishy taste. The fishy taste can be avoided by using a high quality formulation such as OmegaBrite or Coromega or by freezing the capsules prior to ingesting them. Other strategies include taking the capsules with food and splitting the dose to several times daily. There is also a prescription Omega 3 called Lovaza which is FDA approved for treating very high trigylcerides (not depression).

SAM-e: Very minimal side effects in trials

Risks

Omega 3 fatty acids could contain harmful heavy metals such as mercury. It is important to buy from a reliable source.

It is important for patients like Amelia to consider antidepressants if they do not improve with psychotherapy or natural treatments. Inadequately treated depression may lead to suicidal thoughts, increased medical illness (perhaps there is a connection with Amelia's migraines) and an increased risk of substance abuse.

Any sedating medications may increase the likelihood of falls, especially in the elderly.

Resources

Web Sites

National Association of Cognitive Behavioral Therapists
www.nacbt.org

Healthy Minds
www.healthyminds.org

National Institutes of Mental Health
www.nimh.nih.gov/publicat/depression.cfm

National Center for Complementary and Alternative Medicine
www.nccam.nih.gov

Books

Against Depression
Peter D. Kramer
Penguin, 2006

Feeling Good: The New Mood Therapy
David Burns
Avon, 1999

You Can Think Like a Psychiatrist, Second Edition
Leslie Lundt
Foothills Foundation, 2007

The Pill Book Guide to Natural Medicines
Michael Murray
Bantam, 2002

Therapy Types

The best long-term outcomes in mental health result from a combination of therapy and well-managed medications. Psychotherapy, also called counseling, is a practice where you examine your thoughts, feelings, actions and relationships. A trained specialist aids in evaluating problems that exist and where changes are likely to create an improved well being. Below you will find a list of therapies that have shown to be effective both for individuals and families with a variety of diagnoses.

Interpersonal Psychotherapy	The focus of Interpersonal Psychotherapy (IPT) is to explore interpersonal events in the patient's life and develop coping strategies to deal with these events. These events can include relationship conflict, changes in family roles and grief from any number of losses.
Cognitive Behavior Therapy	Cognitive Behavior Therapy (CBT) is a form of psychotherapy that emphasizes the important role of thinking in how we feel and what we do. Through identifying thinking that is causing the feelings and behaviors, the patient learns to replace this thinking with thoughts that lead to more desirable actions.
Group Therapy	Group psychotherapy, like individual psychotherapy, is intended to help people who would like to improve their ability to cope with difficulties and problems in their lives. In group therapy, the patient learns that he or she is not alone in experiencing psychological adjustments problems, and can experiment with trying to relate to people differently in a safe environment. The group can have a specific focus, such as sexual abuse or bereavement, or it can be designed to develop self-esteem, intimacy or trust.
Family Therapy	Family therapy focuses on changes within a family, and recognizes that family relationships have an impact on the feelings, behavior and psychological adjustment of every member. All the family members are involved in the therapy process.
Alcoholics Anonymous	Alcoholics Anonymous (AA) was founded on the belief that recovering alcoholics can help each other stay sober. It is a form of open-ended public group therapy that requires only a desire to stop drinking to attend. Some AA meetings are closed to those who are recovering from alcoholism. Other meetings are open to anyone who is interested in following the outlined 12 steps and traditions. All addiction recovery includes some form of the AA model and meetings are held in communities all around the world.
Couples Therapy	Couples therapy focuses on the problems existing in the relationship between two people. The therapy involves identifying individual problems, as well as the relationship conflicts.
Play Therapy	Play therapists encourage the advancement of the psychosocial development and mental health of people through play and play therapy. Play therapists foster the clients' interest and welfare as well as nurturing relationships in the child's life.

Sources: www.interpersonalpsychotherapy.org/ International Society for Interpersonal Therapy, www.agpa.org American Group Psychotherapy Association, www.nacbt.org National Association of Cognitive Behavioral Therapy, www.a4pt.org National Association for Play Therapy, www.aamft.org American Association of Marriage and Family Therapy, www.apa.org American Psychological Association, www.counseling.org American Counseling Association, www.alcoholics-anonymous.org Alcoholics Anonymous

Case of

Billy Bully

Billy is a 27-year-old engineer who came to the office accompanied by his wife. "We've been married for two years and these past three months his anger and rage are unbearable," reports his wife. "Billy thinks people are stupid. Last week he got in an argument with the gas station attendant for not having the right paper towels." He states he has moved up quickly in the company "because I know how to run this place. People need to get out of my way so I can get things done around here." His friends have been commenting on his relentless phone calls to them at 3 a.m. these past three months. He has spent money on new computers and video editing equipment that his wife said they don't have. His wife says he has never had a problem with alcohol but in the past three months has been drinking a half case of beer a day and recently she found a baggie of marijuana and a bong in the garage.

Family History: Mother and sister treated for depression, Dad "drunk and crazy"

Medical History: Broken collar bone from cycling accident

Medications: None   Substance Use: Smokes pot and drinks beer everyday

What do you do?

Billy's history is validated by his family and his friends. These new behaviors are the key to establish the straightforward description of mania. His alcohol abuse appears to have started after the onset of manic symptoms but we need to rule out other drugs of abuse because their effects can look like mania. Observing the patient over time can help confirm the diagnosis of bipolar disorder.

Diagnosis: Bipolar I mood disorder, acute manic episode

Options

1. Psychotherapy

Right now Billy's perception of himself is bulletproof. The chance for therapy to make a difference in his symptoms is unrealistic. Once he gets treated for this mania and starts to recognize patterns of his disorder, therapy can help develop insight and judgment about his behavior. It also can help him increase his commitment to staying on medications to treat all his symptoms.

2. Mood Stabilizers

The oldest mood stabilizer on the planet is Lithium. It was the first mood-stabilizing agent approved by the FDA and is effective in controlling mania and preventing the recurrence of both manic and depressive episodes. We are not absolutely certain how it works, but it is the gold standard which all the new mood stabilizers are measured. Lithium requires baseline lab tests for complete blood count, electrolyte levels, EKG, and kidney function.

Frequent blood tests establish therapeutic levels of lithium and evaluate the impact of the medication on kidneys and thyroid function. Blood tests also help evaluate adherence to the medications.

3. Anticonvulsant Mood Stabilizers

Anticonvulsants, such as Depakote (divalproex sodium) or Equetro (carbamazepine) also can have mood-stabilizing effects and may be especially useful for difficult-to-treat bipolar episodes. Both have FDA approval for treatment of mania. And like lithium, they require frequent blood tests to ensure therapeutic range. Liver function tests and complete blood counts need to be checked. Lamictal (lamotrigine) is not approved for manic episodes.

4. Atypical Antipsychotics

Zyprexa (olanzapine), Risperdal (risperidone), Seroquel (quetiapine), Abilify (aripiprazole), and Geodon (ziprasidone) are all FDA approved for bipolar mania. These antipsychotic medications have their own unique risks and benefits from sedation to weight gain. They all require monitoring blood sugars because of the possible risk of developing diabetes.

My Choice

A drug toxicology screen should be ordered to rule out drugs of abuse, especially methamphetamine. Evaluate Bill's alcohol and marijuana use. He has a family history of alcoholism and increased his use when he started into this mania.

Lithium carbonate is our choice to treat Bill's manic episode because it has a response rate of 70-80%. Obtain baseline laboratory tests and then start with 300 mg for 3 nights and increase to 600 mg. After one week on medication check lithium levels, kidney function and thyroid. Taking the medication with food can minimize the risk of GI upset.

Sleep is the best medication we can give to a patient in a manic episode. The lithium may create some sedation and help with sleep. We may need to add a long-acting non-benzodiazapine like Ambien CR at 12.50 mg or Lunesta 3 mg to help him get to sleep and stay asleep. Will need to worry about addiction potential!

Likely side effects

Lithium: Nausea, diarrhea, tremor and GI upset, which usually improve over time. Skin rash not unusual.

Risk

Lithium can cause hypothyroidism as well as damage the kidneys. Blood monitoring in imperative.

Resources

Web Sites

Extensive Mental Health Information for Specific Topics
www.psycheducation.org

National Institute of Mental Health
www.nimh.nih.gov

E-Medicine Journal
www.emedicine.com/med/topic229.htm

American Psychiatric Association
www.psych.org/public_info/bipolar.cfm

National Alliance for the Mentally Ill
www.nami.org

Books

Electroboy: A Memoir of Mania
Andy Behrman
Random House, 2003

Manic: A Memoir
by Terri Cheney
Harper Paperbacks, 2009

Brilliant Madness: Living with Manic Depressive Illness
Patty Duke
Bantam, 1997

New Hope for People with Bipolar Disorder: Your Friendly, Authoritative Guide to the Latest in Traditional and Complementary Solutions
Jan Fawcett, Bernard Golden, Nancy Rosenfeld
Three Rivers Press, 2007

Practice Guidelines

Practice Guidelines for Treatment of Patients with Bipolar Disorder
American Psychiatric Association, 2002
www.psychiatryonline.com/pracGuide/pracGuideTopic_8.aspx

Mood Stabilizers

Meds/Labs	Textbook recommendation	TCR's "Let's get real" recommendations	TCR's Reasoning/ Research
Lithium			
Serum level (use these recommendations for Depakote also)	Weekly x4, Monthly x3, then quarterly	After 1 week, then yearly (repeat with dosage changes, clinical or compliance issues, or new side effects)	levels won't change much after they reach steady state unless outside factor intrudes
TSH	Baseline, then yearly	Baseline, 2 weeks, then at 6 months, then yearly	Thyroid issues typically arise 2 wks. to 6 mos. after starting Li
BUN/Creatinine	Baseline, then yearly	Baseline, 2 weeks, then yearly	Better to check this after starting Li than before– awaiting baseline delays treatment
EKG	Baseline, then yearly	Not needed for most patients, those with cardiac history should tell primary care provider they are taking Li	Small incidence of bradycardia due to sinus node dysfunction– requires more than EKG for evaluation
Depakote			
Serum level	Same recommendations as for Lithium (see above)		
LFTs	Baseline, then monthly x 6, then Q 6 mos.	After 2 weeks, then yearly, unless symptoms of hepatitis	Hepatotoxicity almost unheard of in patients over the age of 2; mild increase in LFTs more common, usually benign, reversible
CBC	Baseline, then monthly x 6, then Q 6 mos.	After 2 weeks, then at 6 months, then yearly (unless easy bruising)—more vigilance in elderly	Significant thrombocytopenia rare in large studies; elderly may be more at risk
Tegretol/Equetro			
Serum level	Q 2 weeks x 3 mos., then quarterly	At 1 week, 1 month, then yearly (repeat with dosage changes, clinical or compliance issues, or new side effects)	Because of auto-induction, level at 1 month is useful, but no further induction expected afterwards
CBC	Baseline, then Q two wks. x 2, monthly x 3, quarterly	After 1 week, 1 month, 3 months, then yearly	Occurrence of leukopenia rare, occurs within 1 month
Sodium	Baseline, then yearly	After 1 week, then yearly	Uncommon side effect
LFTs	Baseline, then Q two weeks x 4, then quarterly	After 2 weeks, then yearly, unless symptoms of hepatitis	Actual hepatitis very rare

TCR = The Carlat Report

Adapted from The Carlat Report on Psychiatric Treatment (www.TheCarlatReport.com), 2007, Volume 5 Number 8. © Clearview Publishing 2007. Used with permission.

Case of

Daniel Darkmood

Daniel is a 45-year-old policeman referred by his family doctor. Reluctant to come to a "shrink's" office, he says he needs to do something to get out of the "funk" he's had for nearly a year. He reports, "I've had a few bad days in the past, but never this many in a row. On days off I'd stay in bed all day if I didn't have to walk the dog and take my wife to work." He states that his thoughts are "smothered" and that his lack of focus and concentration is getting in the way of his confidence at work. Daniel is tearful as he offers, "My wife has stopped asking me to go places, we haven't had sex in months. I have a garage full of toys that I'd just as soon sell. I'm supposed to be a big tough cop and suck it up, but look at me. I'm in a shrink's office."

Family History: Mother treated for depression. Maternal grandfather killed himself when his mom was 16.

Medical History: Broken ankle from college football

Substance Use: On days off, 4-6 beers   Medications: None

What do you do?

For many men, depression carries so much shame that it is often hidden. As a result, it is vastly underdiagnosed. Their shame at having feelings inconsistent with the male role can silence them. They suffer a compound depression; they are depressed about feeling depressed.

Diagnosis: Major depression, single episode

Now what?

1. Psychotherapy

Therapy can help Daniel regain a sense of control and pleasure in life. It can help him see choices as well as gradually incorporate enjoyable and fulfilling activities. Daniel is in a very high risk line of work and post traumatic stress disorder (PTSD) needs to be ruled out. Couples therapy would create an arena for Daniel and his wife to establish goals for their marriage and regain trust.

2. SSRI

The late 1980s started the ball rolling for a new class of antidepressants called SSRIs (selective serotonin reuptake inhibitors). Their serotonin selectivity creates different side effects as well as a higher safety profile than previously available antidepressants. Prozac (fluoxetine), Zoloft (sertraline), Paxil (paroxetine), Celexa (citalopram) and Lexapro (escitalopram) are all approved for depression. Lexapro is the latest addition to the SSRI family. Even though they share the same serotonin properties they all have their own unique strengths and side effects.

3. SNRI

Effexor XR (venlafaxine) and Cymbalta (duloxetine) are serotonin and norepinephrine reuptake inhibitors (SNRI) that work on both serotonin and norepinephrine to treat depression. They are approved for major depressive disorder in adults. Cymbalta claims to treat the aches and pains that can accompany depression. The new kids on the block are Pristiq (desvenlafaxine) and Savella (milnacipran). Savella is only approved for fibromyalgia.

4. Wellbutrin XL (bupropion)

Wellbutrin XL (bupropion) is in a class of its own. It is FDA approved for depression and targets dopamine and norepinephrine. Dopamine and norepinephrine are recognized for energy, focus and motivation. Because it targets these neurotransmitters, Wellbutrin XL can be more stimulating. It can not be used with anyone who has history of an eating disorder, seizure or head injury. While there are rare reported sexual side effects, it can increase blood pressure and disrupt sleep.

My Choice

Begin Wellbutrin XL, starting at 150 mg each morning and in one week check response and side effects. We want to match Daniel's symptoms of low motivation, sleeping too much and loss of focus and concentration with the medication. He has no history of seizure or head injury.

We need to address Daniel's beer consumption. It is a depressant and may interfere with the response of the Wellbutrin XL.

Helping him recognize the risk and benefits of all treatment strategies is very important and we would see him at least weekly until we ensure response with no increase in blood pressure or insomnia. He has a strong family history of depression and a very stressful job so therapy is important to help normalize this experience and rule out PTSD. Couples therapy will also help him and his wife get back on track.

Likely side effects

Wellbutrin XL: Weight loss, headache, agitation, sweating, and tremor.

Risks

All medications for depression carry a warning about the potential of increasing suicidal/homicidal ideation.

Daniel needs to be aware of the risks and benefits of the medication and he needs to be monitored closely the first few weeks of treatment.

Resources

Web Sites

Real Men, Real Depression
www.menanddepression.nimh.nih.gov/

Men's Health and Depression
www.menshealth.about.com/od/psychologicalissues/a/depression.htm

Male Depression Support
www.maledepression.com

Books

I Don't Want to Talk About It: Overcoming the Secret Legacy of Male Depression
Terrance Real
Scribner Press, 1998

Is He Depressed or What?: What to Do When the Man You Love Is Irritable, Moody, And Withdrawn
by David B. Wexler
New Harbinger Publications, 2006

Lifting the Weight: Understanding Depression in Men, Its Causes and Solutions
by Martin Kantor
Praeger Publishers, 2007

Practice Guidelines

Practice Guideline for the Treatment of Patients with Major Depressive Disorder
2nd Edition. American Psychiatric Association, 2000
www.psychiatryonline.com/pracGuide/pracGuideTopic_7.aspx

Case of
Brooke Blue

Brooke is a 33-year-old woman 12 weeks postpartum referred by her obstetrician. "Having a baby was the happiest day of my life," she reports, "but lately I can't seem to shake these horrible feelings and I think I'm losing it." Since she has been breastfeeding she has not had more than four hours of sleep at one time and resents that her husband's life has not changed at all. She has a constant headache, has lost 15 pounds, eats "because I have to," and says most days she "goes through the motions." She has been irritable, refuses to answer the telephone, is avoiding friends and feels guilty that she can't get things done.

Family History: Mother started on Zoloft in menopause.

Substance Use: Coffee 2-3 cups each morning   Medications: None

---

What to do?

It is a myth that pregnancy and motherhood is always a happy, glowing experience. Approximately 85 percent of women experience some type of mood disorder during the postpartum period. About 10-15 percent develop symptoms of depression and anxiety that are far more significant.

Postpartum depression can affect anyone regardless of education or socioeconomic status. Risk factors that have been identified: Previous episode of postpartum depression, depression during pregnancy, history of depression, recent stressful event, inadequate social support, and marital problems.

Diagnosis: Major depression, postpartum onset

Options

1. No medications—psychotherapy and support group

Therapy can support Brooke to explore her own needs, attitudes and beliefs without feeling pressure from others. It can help normalize the feelings she faces during this major transition in her life. A support group would also help Brooke by connecting her with others experiencing the same feelings. Support for the rest of the family is important as well because they may be the first to recognize changes in Brooke's mood.

2. Start SSRI

Prozac (fluoxetine), Zoloft (sertraline), and Paxil (paroxetine), Lexapro (escitalopram), and Celexa (citalopram) are all FDA approved for major depression. They work in the serotonin pathway and have shown to be effective in treating symptoms related to postpartum depression.

3. Start SNRI

Effexor XR, (venlafaxine), Pristiq (desvenlafaxine) and Cymbalta (duloxetine) are antidepressants that work in both the serotonin and norepinephrine pathways. They are all approved for major depression. Savella (milnacipran) is the newest of the class, but only FDA approved for fibromyalgia.

4. Start bupropion

Wellbutrin XL (bupropion) has a different mechanism of action than the other antidepressants.

My Choice

Since Brooke is breastfeeding she must weigh the risks and benefits of starting an antidepressant. All medications are secreted into breast milk; however, the amount of medication the baby is exposed to appears to be relatively small. How much drug the baby is exposed to depends on the medication dosage as well as age and feeding schedule. It has not been established that any antidepressant medication has been associated with serious adverse events in the baby yet fluoxetine and citalopram are at the bottom of the list. The American Journal of Psychiatry and the New England Journal of Medicine data point to Zoloft (sertraline) as the drug of choice. We would start Brooke on Zoloft for 2 days then increase to 50 mg, increasing by 25 mg every 4 days to an effective dose (max dose 200 mg).

Refer both Brooke and her husband for psychotherapy and a support group. Depression can interfere with the very important mother-infant bonding that starts during pregnancy. The long-term consequences for a disruption in this bonding are well studied and have shown to contribute to later cognitive and behavioral deficits in the child.

Likely side effects

Zoloft: Nausea, possibly anxiety at first and ongoing sexual side effects including decreased libido and difficulty with orgasm. In general, the risk of adverse events in the nursing infant appears to be low but collaboration with the child's pediatrician is essential. Monitor the baby for any changes in sleep and eating patterns, behavior and level of alertness.

Risks

SSRIs can prompt suicidal and homicidal ideation. While this is rare it is important to monitor Brooke weekly in the first months of treatment.

Resources

Web Sites

Postpartum Education for Parents
www.sbpep.org

www.postpartum.net
Postpartum Support International

Books

Down Came The Rain: My Journey Through Postpartum Depression
Brooke Shields
Hyperion, 2006

Beyond the Blues: A Guide to Understanding And Treating Prenatal And Postpartum Depression
by Shoshana S. Bennett and Pec Indman
Moodswing Press, 2006

This Isn't What I Expected: Overcoming Postpartum Depression
Karen Kleiman and Valerie Raskin
Bantam Books, 1995

Journal Articles

Altshuler LL, et al. (2001). The expert consensus guideline series: Treatment of depression in women. *Postgraduate Medicine Special Report* (March): 1–116, 2001.

Stowe, Z (2007). The use of mood stabilizers during breastfeeding. *J Clin Psychiatry*; 68 (supp 9):22-28.

Meltzer-Brody, Samantha, et al. (2008). Postpartum depression: What to tell patients who breast-feed. *Current Psychiatry* ; 7(5).

Treatment of Postpartum Depression, Part Two. *J Clinical Psychiatry* 2004; 65(9):1252-65.

Case of
Frustrated Fred

Fred is a 55-year-old retired fireman. His daughter arrives at the office with him and explains. "Dad has always had a temper, and now he is a mean old man. If he is not frustrated and angry he is home by himself with the telephone off the hook. The grandkids don't even want to be with him. Since his last wife left him (married four times) he has had three speeding tickets and his neighbors called the cops on him last week when he was yelling at the garbage collector for being late." Fred interrupts, "I was in a hurry to get somewhere and there was no traffic around. It's no big deal. America has turned into a prison and my telephone and mail campaign is going to change the way we live." Fred admits he is sleeping only three or four hours a night because he is working on his campaign and states he is not at all tired. On questioning, Fred says he has had episodes of highs and lows since high school. In the military he was reprimanded for his temper and released early with an honorable discharge. His daughter said Fred "hates doctors and I had to threaten him to get him to come with me today."

Family History: Father committed suicide, alcoholism

Medical History: Gall bladder surgery age 38

Substance Use: 4-5 drinks a day, smokes 1 pack per day, 2-3 cups coffee

Medications: ASA

What do you do?

Bipolar disorder is often not recognized; people suffer for years before it is diagnosed and treated. Like diabetes or heart disease, bipolar disorder is a long-term illness needing careful management throughout a person's life. Symptoms of bipolar disorder can be a moving target and need to be observed over time to confirm the diagnosis. In the meantime we need to treat Fred's symptoms.

Diagnosis: Bipolar disorder, recent manic episode
Alcohol abuse/dependence

Options

1. Rule out other physical conditions

At age 55 Fred needs an age-appropriate complete physical exam and medical work-up. Include a neurological work-up to rule out dementia or stroke.

2. Psychotherapy

Right now Fred is resistant to treatment and is being dragged to the doctor by his daughter. He has a family history of alcoholism and suicide and he may be headed down that same path. Over time he will benefit from interpersonal and group therapy and start to recognize the triggers and patterns of his mood swings and the part alcohol has played in them.

3. Mood stabilizer—Anticonvulsants

The cluster of Fred's symptoms: irritability, impulsiveness, grandiosity and decreased need for sleep require a mood stabilizer. Equetro (carbamazepine) and Depakote (divalproex sodium) have FDA indications for bipolar mania. They require blood tests to monitor levels of the medication, liver function and complete blood counts. Lamictal (lamotrigine) is an anticonvulsant that has been effective in treating the depressive symptoms without requiring ongoing blood monitoring.

4. Mood stabilizer—Atypical antipsychotics

Risperdal (risperidone), Zyprexa (olanzapine), Geodon (ziprasidone), Abilify (aripiprazole), and Seroquel (quetiapine) all have FDA approval for bipolar mania. They all have their own unique side effects and they all act very quickly to interrupt the symptoms of mania.

My Choice

Fred's daughter described a progression of his shifts in behavior over his lifetime. True to bipolar mania, his ideas of grandeur and impulsive behavior have been consistent over time.

Make sure Fred gets a full medical work-up to rule out any medical problems. Because it works quickly, we will start Fred on Risperdal 0.5 mg at night and see him again in 2-3 days and then at least weekly until his symptoms improve. By seeing him frequently we can adjust the Risperdal to improve his sleep as well as his mood and irritability and monitor any side effects. Have him start a diary to track his moods.

Address Fred's alcohol use. He is genetically set up for abuse, but many times an untreated patient treats himself with alcohol. The medications cannot work well in the presence of alcohol and we need a strong commitment from him to eliminate it. We may need to start Campral (acamprosate) to help with protracted alcohol withdrawal symptoms.

Likely side effects

Risperdal: Sedation, dizziness, constipation. Monitor weight.

Risks

Lab monitoring is recommended to follow blood sugars and lipids with Risperdal and all atypical antipsychotics.

Resources

Web Sites

National Institute of Mental Health
www.nimh.nih.gov

Real Men Real Depression
www.menanddepression.nimh.nih.gov

The Center for Reintegration
www.reintegration.com/ami/bipolar/symptoms.asp

Depression and Bipolar Support Alliance
www.dbsalliance.org

Books

What Goes up . . . Surviving the Manic Episode of a Loved One
Judy Eron
Barricade Books, 2005

The Bipolar Workbook: Tools for Controlling Your Mood Swings
Monica Ramirez Basco
Guilford Press, 2005

New Hope for People with Bipolar Disorder
Jan Fawcett, Bernard Golden, and Nancy Rosenfeld
Three Rivers Press, 2007

An Unquiet Mind: A Memoir of Moods and Madness
Kay Redfield Jamison
Vintage Press, 1997

Practice Guidelines

Treatment of Patients with Bipolar Disorder, Second Edition
www.psychiatryonline.com/pracGuide/pracGuideChapToc_8.aspx

Antipsychotics Approved for Bipolar Disorder

Medication	Approved for...	Starting Dose	Target Dose
Zyprexa	1. Manic episode 2. Combo with Li or Depakote 3. Maintenance	10-15mg qD	10-20mg qD
Risperdal	1. Manic or mixed episode 2. Combo with Li or Depakote	2-3mg BID	2-3mg qD
Seroquel	1. Manic episode 2. Combo with Li or Depakote 3. Bipolar depression	50mg BID	400-800mg qD
Geodon	Manic or mixed episode	40mg BID	60mg BID
Abilify	Manic or mixed episode Maintenance	10mg qD	15-30mg qD

Adapted from The Carlat Report on Psychiatric Treatment (www.TheCarlatReport.com), 2005, Volume 3, Number 2. Copyright © Clearview Publishing 2005. Used with permission.

Case of

Polarized Perry

Perry is a 22-year-old college senior sent to the clinic by his student health service. For the past three weeks he has been destructive and disorderly in his dorm. He is shouting out his window at students passing by, and has started a campaign to have marijuana approved for use in his dorm. He writes numerous articles for the school newspaper and appears on the college radio and television stations. He reports a strong following and feels confident the school will change its policy. He has a diagnosis of bipolar disorder and stopped taking lithium two months ago. "I hate taking pills morning and night. The diarrhea stinks and sometimes my hands shake so bad I can't even type." He says he started lithium his first year of college and stayed on it only to please his mom.

Family History: Uncle bipolar, Mom and sister treated for depression

Medical History: Hospitalized first manic episode ,

Medications: None

Substance Use: Smokes pot 2-3 times a day, drinks alcohol 2-3 times a week

What do you do?

Stopping medications is an age-old pattern for patients with a diagnosis of bipolar. As a college student living in a dorm, Perry is in the midst of the chaos of busy schedules, inconsistent sleep times, poor diet and high doses of sex, drugs and rock 'n' roll. Researchers stress the need for early and aggressive treatment to prevent the brain from "kindling" and going into rapid cycling or becoming treatment resistant.

> **Diagnosis: Bipolar Disorder I, recent episode manic**
> **Marijuana and alcohol abuse**

Options

1. Psychotherapy

Therapy can help increase a commitment to medications and a balanced lifestyle. A full blown mania in a 22-year-old male does not lend itself to good insight and judgment, and Perry does not see the devastation created by his untreated disorder. Once his mood is stabilized he can start recognizing the patterns that can either support or sabotage his treatment.

2. Drug testing and complete physical

Perry admits to smoking marijuana every day and drinking alcohol every week. We need to rule out any other drugs of abuse that can mimic bipolar mania.

3. Mood Stabilizer—Lithium

Lithium was the only bipolar treatment available for a long time. The side effects that do not resolve over time can be unmanageable. Lithium is a salt and requires attention to fluid intake as well as blood work to monitor medication levels and side effects.

4. Mood Stabilizer—Anticonvulsants

Lamictal (lamotrigine) is an anticonvulsant that has been effective in treating the depressive symptoms of bipolar disorder without ongoing blood monitoring. After lithium, Depakote (divalproex sodium) was the second mood stabilizer approved by the FDA for bipolar mania. Equetro (carbamazepine) also has FDA approval. They require blood tests to monitor levels of the medication, liver function and complete blood counts.

5. Mood Stabilizer—Atypical Antipsychotics

In the past five years Zyprexa (olanzapine), Risperdal (risperidone), Abilify (aripiprazole), Geodon (ziprasidone), and Seroquel (quetiapine) have received FDA approval for treating bipolar mania. They all have shown efficacy with their own distinctive side effects.

My Choice

Sleep deprivation and substance abuse are precipitants of bipolar cycling and need to be addressed immediately. The dorm may not be the best place for him to live. Depakote can be dosed one time a day. We will start at 500 mg for 4 nights and then check blood levels. If Perry is not willing to be seen several times a week until his symptoms are managed he will need to be hospitalized. During this intensive treatment time the education begins again and eventually Perry will learn to be an expert in managing his care.

Likely side effects

Depakote: Nausea, drowsiness, tremor, dizziness—all can be minimized if taken at night. In women, worry about development of polycystic ovarian syndrome.

Risks

Depakote can infrequently cause liver problems and low platelet count. Blood work is necessary to monitor these risks, as well as to maintain therapeutic blood levels.

Resources

Web Sites

National Institute of Mental Health
www.nimh.nih.gov/health/publications/bipolar-disorder/complete-index.shtml

National Association for Mental Illness
www.nami.org

http://psychguides.com/Bipolar%20Handout.pdf
Treatment of Bipolar Disorder: A Guide for Patients and Families

Bipolar Central
www.psycom.net/depression.central.bipolar.html

Books

Loving Someone with Bipolar Disorder
by Julie A. Fast and John D. Preston
New Harbinger Publications, 2004

Take Charge of Bipolar Disorder: A 4-Step Plan for You and Your Loved Ones to Manage the Illness and Create Lasting Stability
by Julie A Fast and John Preston
Warner Wellness, 2006

Practice Guidelines

Practice Guidelines for Treatment of Patients with Bipolar Disorder, 2nd edition
www.psychiatryonline.com/pracGuide/pracGuideChapToc_8.aspx

Case of

Herman Heartache

Herman is a 55-year-old male referred by his cardiologist for depression and anxiety. Six months ago he suffered a major heart attack. He had stents placed in two coronary arteries and spent nearly a week in intensive care stabilizing his blood pressure and heart rate. Herman reports feeling like life is not worth living anymore. He has not been sleeping because he is afraid he won't wake up and naps during the day in front of the television. Herman's wife has encouraged him to start a cardiac rehab program but he is afraid to exercise for fear his symptoms of chest pain will return and he'll have another heart attack and die. He has been afraid to return to work because of poor concentration and difficulty making decisions and thinks he should retire.

Family History: Father died of heart attack age 60. No history of mental health problems until now.

Medical History: Heart attack, high cholesterol and high blood pressure

Substance Use: 1-2 Gin and tonics on weekend

Medications: Verapamil (calcium channel blocker), Captopril (ACE inhibitor), Crestor (statin)

Studies have shown that depressed patients are more likely than non-depressed patients to die of a subsequent cardiac problem after being hospitalized for a heart attack. After a heart attack, 20 percent to 25 percent of patients develop major depression, but it often goes untreated. (American Heart Association Journal, August 12, 2003)

Diagnosis: Major depressive disorder, single episode

Options

1. No medications—Cognitive Behavior Therapy (CBT)

Once heart disease develops, it requires lifelong management. Herman needs to be assessed and monitored for suicide as he reports that life is not worth living any more. Depression may make it harder to take the medications needed and to carry out the treatment for preventing another heart attack. Cognitive behavior therapy may help promote adherence to medication and self care.

2. Treat with SSRI

SSRI medications target serotonin and are FDA approved to treat depression. All SSRIs have side effects ranging from agitation to sedation. They also have the potential for harmful interactions with other classes of medications.

3. Treat with Wellbutrin XL (bupropion)

Wellbutrin XL targets dopamine and norepinephrine and is FDA approved for treatment of depression. Potential side effects of Wellbutrin XL are an increase in blood pressure, headache and disrupted sleep.

4. Treat with Effexor XR (venlafaxine) or Pristiq or Cymbalta (duloxetine)

These medications target two chemicals, serotonin and norepinephrine, and are approved by the FDA for depression. The potential for drug interactions with this class is minimized by using Pristiq. All of these medications require blood pressure monitoring.

5. Non-benzodiazepine for sleep

Ambien/Ambien CR (zolpidem) and Lunesta (eszopiclone) are short-acting hypnotics that have been approved for insomnia. These medications also have low drug interactions and can increase total sleep time and perhaps decrease daytime naps.

My Choice

Start Lexapro, an SSRI, 10mg qD. With the heart medications Herman takes it is important to minimize the risk of drug interactions. Lexapro has a favorable drug interaction profile and most patients tolerate it very well. Wellbutrin XL, Effexor XR, Pristiq and Cymbalta all have risk of increasing blood pressure which would be contraindicated with Herman's medical history. We would also add Lunesta (if his insomnia persists) to increase total sleep time.

Herman also needs to start therapy. Heart disease is something that requires major life changes, not just for Herman, but for his entire family. Also encourage Herman to get involved in a cardiac rehab program where he can exercise in a safe and medically controlled environment and meet others with similar experiences.

Likely side effects

SSRIs can create sexual side effects like decreased libido and delayed ejaculation.

Risks

SSRIs can trigger homicidal and/or suicidal ideation. This is quite uncommon, but patients starting on antidepressants need to be monitored weekly during the first months of treatment.

Resources

Web Sites

American Heart Association
www.americanheart.org

Books

Thriving With Heart Disease: The Leading Authority on the Emotional Effects of Heart Disease Tells You and Your Family How to Heal and Reclaim Your Lives
Wayne Sotile and Robin Cantor-Cooke
Free Press, 2004

The Healthy Heart Miracle: Your Roadmap to Lifelong Health
Gabe Mirkin
HarperTorch, 2006

Heart Disease for Dummies
James Rippe
For Dummies, 2004

The First Year: Heart Disease: An Essential Guide for the Newly Diagnosed
Lawrence D. Chilnick
Da Capo, 2008

The Cardiac Recovery Handbook: The Complete Guide to Life After Heart Attack or Heart Surgery, Second Edition
Paul Kligfield
Hatherleigh, 2006

Journal Articles

Depression and Risk of Sudden Cardiac Death and Coronary Heart Disease in Women
J Am Coll Cardiol (2009); 53:950-958

Case of

Lonely Loni

Loni, a 16-year-old girl, is referred by her pediatrician. During her otherwise normal annual physical exam, Loni began crying. When asked why, she stated that no one likes her and she has never had a boyfriend. She has gained 20 pounds since her last exam. Since the black box warning on SSRIs in children was announced, Dr. Nicely refers all of her depressed children to a psychiatrist.

Loni's grades have fallen from A's to C's this year. She quit the volleyball team and does not socialize with her friends. She prefers black clothes and now wears heavy black makeup. Instead of listening to U2 (she was a huge Bono fan in 9th grade), she plays Nirvana continuously.

Family History: Older sister struggled with depression as an adolescent. Grandmother was institutionalized after giving birth to Loni's mother.

Medical History: Negative

Medications: Birth control pills for menstrual irregularities

What do you do?

Loni has classical symptoms of adolescent depression: she has lost interest in activities, her grades have dropped, her mood is down, her clothing and musical tastes have changed dramatically. She denies any precipitating events, but we must be alert for evidence of recent undisclosed trauma. She denies active suicidal ideation, but states she has no reason to live.

Diagnosis: Major depression, single episode

Options

1. No medications—psychotherapy only

Loni has multiple psychosocial issues which could be helped with therapy that focuses on peer relationships, self esteem and body image.

2. Treat with SSRIs

The only medication approved for depression in both children and adolescents is Prozac (fluoxetine). Lexapro (escitalopram) was recently approved for children 12 to 17 years old.

3. Give another antidepressant such as Effexor XR, Pristiq, or Cymbalta

Effexor XR (venlafaxine), Pristiq (desvenlafaxine) and Cymbalta (duloxetine) are NSRIs. They inhibit reuptake of norepinephrine and serotonin. These have not been approved for use in children nor adolescents.

4. Treat with a tricyclic antidepressant that is indicated for adolescents

TCAs are rarely used in adolescents due to the risk of cardiac problems and overdose potential. Regular EKGs must be performed to monitor QTc intervals.

My Choice

I prefer a combination of psychotherapy and medications in patients such as Loni. Prozac is an excellent choice for adolescent girls—not only is it the only approved antidepressant for this age group but we find it unlikely to cause weight gain. Another advantage is that it has a long half-life, meaning that it stays in one's system for a long time before being metabolized. In practice, this results in significantly less discontinuation symptoms if doses are skipped. The FDA has suggested that children and adolescents starting on antidepressants be seen weekly for medication checks.

Likely side effects

Stomach upset, mild anxiety and sleep disturbances are not uncommon when first starting Prozac.

Risks

SSRIs are rarely associated with suicidal/homicidal ideation even without pre-existing depression. Loni needs to be monitored closely during the first several weeks of treatment. A detailed risk/benefit discussion with Loni's parents is necessary and needs to be documented in the medical record.

Resources

Web Sites

American Psychiatric Association
www.healthyminds.org/childrenmentalillnessmedicine.cfm

Musicians for Mental health
www.mpoweryouth.org/411.htm

Federal Drug Administration
www.fda.gov/Cder/drug/antidepressants/MG_template.pdf
FDA's medication guide about using antidepressants in children and teenagers

Guide for patients and families about medications for depression
www.parentsmedguide.org

Books

Feeling Terrific: Four Strategies for Overcoming Depression Using Mood Regulation Therapy
Namir Damluji, Michele Downey, and Renee Sievert
iUniverse, 2005

Recovering from Depression: A Workbook for Teens
Mary Ellen Copeland and Stuart Copans
Brookes, 2002

Beyond the Blues: A Workbook to Help Teens Overcome Depression
Lisa M. Schab
Instant Help books, 2008

Adolescent Depression: A Guide for Parents
Francis Mark Mondimore
Johns Hopkins University Press, 2002

When Nothing Matters Anymore: A Survival Guide for Depressed Teens
Bev Cobain (Kurt's mother)
Free Spirit Publishing, 2007

Case of
Marilyn Moodswinger—1

Marilyn is a 28-year-old woman referred by her family nurse practitioner. On her last visit to her nurse practitioner she arrived wearing bright pink clothing, shoes, hose, lipstick that matched her clothing and heavy eye make-up. Her husband reports that the night before she had been to a bar with her friends, bought everyone drinks and claimed she was a millionaire. He states she has been very irritable and has been making calls to corporations asking for their financial support to run for public office. She has slept only two or three hours a night for the past two weeks. During the night she has been walking on her treadmill or at the computer in chat rooms trying to gain support for her political campaign. She states she has been depressed most of her life and at last she feels better.

Family History: Aunt was hospitalized for "acting crazy." Mother and sister treated with medications for depression.

Medical History: Sprained ankles from gymnastics

Medications: Oral Contraceptives, Multivitamin

Substance Use: Marilyn reports "rarely drinks," husband reports in past month has been drinking 2-3 gin and tonics each night.

What do you do?

Mood swings ranging from intense euphoria to profound depression are symptoms of bipolar mood disorder. Marilyn reports she has never felt better and has little or no insight that her behaviors are inappropriate. Since this is the first manic episode it is imperative to get a complete family history and input from friends and family that have known Marilyn a long time.

> ## Diagnosis: Bipolar I Disorder, acute manic episode

Options

1. Mood Stabilizers—anticonvulsants

Depakote (divalproex), Equetro (carbamazepine) and Lamictal (lamotrigine) have all been FDA approved as mood stabilizers. Depakote and Equetro both have been shown effective for treating acute mania. Depakote requires blood tests to monitor potential liver problems, and Equetro requires blood tests to monitor for blood dyscrasias such as anemia and agranulocytosis. Lamictal requires slow titration to minimize the risk of developing serious rashes; it has been found particularly effective for the depressive component of bipolar disorder.

2. Mood Stabilizers—Atypical Antipsychotics

Zyprexa (olanzapine), Risperdal (risperidone), Seroquel (quetiapine), Geodon (ziprasidone) and Abilify (aripiprazole) all have FDA approval for acute mania in the bipolar client. All of these medications have a rapid onset, and each has its own side effects profile.

3. Lithium

Lithium is approved by the FDA for acute mania and has been shown to prevent or diminish the intensity of further manic episodes. It requires very close blood monitoring to minimize the risk of toxicity to kidneys and thyroid.

4. Address substance use

Cocaine, methamphetamines, and PCP can mimic symptoms of mania. Consuming these drugs and excess alcohol can be part of the high-risk behaviors related to mania.

5. No medications—psychotherapy alone

Eventually the client with bipolar mood disorder can benefit from psychotherapy to help develop insight into patterns of behavior and build coping strategies for dealing with a chronic disease. Because problems can surface as a result of this chronic disorder, the entire family needs education and ongoing support.

My Choice

While it is imperative we treat this manic episode aggressively, we need to educate Marilyn and her family about maintenance treatment for this disorder as well. Most bipolar patients are on 2-3 medications for maintenance therapy. We would start Marilyn on Geodon 80 mg day one, increasing to 80 mg AM and 40 mg PM on day two. Dose would be titrated to 80 mg twice a day if needed. Mood stabilizers are first line medications for clients with bipolar mania. While all the mood stabilizers would most likely target her symptoms, Geodon has less risk of weight gain and is less sedating than many of the other choices.

During an episode of mania, Marilyn's insight and judgment are impaired and she needs ongoing support from her family. Psychotherapy will be most valuable when she recovers from the manic episode. We would refer Marilyn and her family to the local NAMI group and individual counseling.

Side effects

Geodon—Sedation and dizziness

Risks

Geodon has shown in very rare cases to slow down cardiac conduction. We need to rule out any cardiac history and perform a routine baseline ECG.

Resources

Web Sites

National Institute of Mental Health
www.nimh.nih.gov/

www.psycheducation.org
Extensive mental health information for specific topics

E-Medicine Journal
www.emedicine.com/med/topic229.htm

Tools for Clinicians
www.manicdepressive.org/tools_clinical.html
www.measurecme.org

Research on Bipolar Disorder
www.stepbd.org

Books

Treatment of Bipolar Illness: A Casebook of Clinicians and Patients
Gabriele Leverich and Robert Post
W.W. Norton and Co., 2008

Manic-Depressive Illness: Bipolar Disorders and Recurrent Depression,
2nd Edition
Frederick K. Goodwin and Kay Redfield Jamison
Oxford University Press, 2007

Cognitive-Behavioral Therapy for Bipolar Disorder, Second Edition
Monica Ramirez Basco and A. John Rush
Guilford Press, 2007

Break the Bipolar Cycle: A Day-by-Day Guide to Living with Bipolar Disorder
Elizabeth Brondolo and Xavier Amador
McGraw-Hill, 2007

Marilyn Moodswinger—2

Remember Marilyn? She was the 28-year-old woman who arrived at the office in a manic episode and was diagnosed with bipolar disorder. She is back in the office with complaints of "never felt this bad in my life, and if this is as good as it gets I'm stopping the medication right now." Since starting the Geodon she has not had any episodes of mania and is sleeping eight or nine hours a night. She states she doesn't have any energy and is dragging herself through the day "I miss the excitement, energy and intensity I had before." Her husband states she has not been to work in the past two weeks, and has refused any kind of therapy because "therapy is for crazy people."

Medications: Geodon 80 mg AM and PM, Oral Contraceptives, Multivitamin

Substance Use: Has started smoking and denies alcohol

What do we do now?

One of the most important factors in treating bipolar disorder is to fully treat all phases of the illness. The manic or high end of Marilyn's mood swings have been managed with the Geodon, but it is not treating the depression or low end of her mood swings. Although mania is the most dramatic phase of the disorder, bipolar depression is more chronic and common.

> **Diagnosis: Bipolar I Disorder, most recent episode depressed.**

Options

1. Psychotherapy

Marilyn has been reluctant to try therapy. It can serve as support while she learns to recognize signs of relapse and intervene before a full-blown illness episode occurs. Interpersonal therapy helps people learn to cope with the challenges of living with a chronic disease, come to terms with changes in self-image and life goals. Group therapy will connect Marilyn with others having the same experience and help her understand the effects the illness has on important relationships.

2. Lithium

Lithium was the first mood-stabilizing agent approved by the FDA. Significant research supports a therapeutic action for acute mania and for protection from recurrence of both manic and depressive episodes. While effective, it requires blood work for lithium levels, and monitor thyroid, kidney function and EKG.

3. Lamictal

Lamictal is the first FDA-approved therapy since lithium for the long-term maintenance of bipolar I disorder. For someone like Marilyn who has been effectively treated for acute manic episodes, it helps treat the other end of the bipolar mood spectrum including depression, recurrent mania, hypomania, and mixed episodes. Most psychiatrists feel Lamictal has robust efficacy in treating bipolar depression.

4. Symbyax

Symbyax is the only antidepressant approved by the FDA for bipolar depression. This medication is a combination of two drugs, olanzapine (an atypical antipsychotic aka Zyprexa) and fluoxetine (aka Prozac - an SSRI). It has been used with some success, although it carries the risk of weight gain and increased cholesterol and triglycerides. Many physicians (myself included) feel restricted by using fixed dose combinations of two readily available meds.

My Choice

Most bipolar patients are on 2-3 different medications to treat their full range of symptoms. Keeping mood stabilization and maintenance in mind as well as drug interactions, we would start Lamictal 25 mg at night for 14 days and increase to 50 mg for 14 days then increase to 100 mg. Lamictal, if tolerated, will be increased up to 200 mg per day. Continue Geodon at current doses to decrease the risk of returning to mania.

We would also make sure Marilyn has a full medical workup to rule out problems with her thyroid, as hypothyroidism can create some of these symptoms.

Marilyn is self treating her depression with nicotine. Discuss the risks to her mood of cigarettes vs. the benefits of smoking. In her mania she was exercising to excess. Encourage her to return to a more moderate exercise regimen.

Reinforce to Marilyn the importance of keeping a mood diary and getting involved in individual and group therapy. Coach her in the expectation that she can become the expert in her care when she understands the diagnosis and treatment regimens.

Side effects

Sedation, nausea, dizziness can all occur with Lamictal.

Risks

Lamictal has a very rare risk of developing a life-threatening rash called Stevens- Johnson. Titrating very slowly is the key to avoiding this problem. Advise patients not to try new cosmetics, shampoo, detergents when starting Lamictal – if they develop a rash it will be unclear if it is the product or the medicine.

Resources

Web Sites

Depression and Bipolar Support Alliance (DBSA)
www.dbsalliance.org
The DBSA offers support, information, and resources for people living with an illness like bipolar disorder. It is also a good source of information for your
family or loved ones.

National Alliance for the Mentally Ill (NAMI)
www.nami.org
NAMI is a nonprofit support advocacy group for people with mental illness. There may be state or local NAMI groups in your area.

www.bipolardepressioninfo.com

Books

Antipsychotics and Mood Stabilizers: Stahl's Essential Psychopharmacology, 3rd edition
Stephen M. Stahl
Cambridge University Press, 2008

Bipolar Depression: A Comprehensive Guide
Rif S. El-Mallakh and S. Nassir Ghaemi
American Psychiatric Publishing, 2006

Case of

Mike Moody

Mike is a 48-year-old attorney referred by his physician assistant and accompanied to the office by his wife. His wife explains, "If he's not frustrated and yelling at me and the kids, he's off by himself not wanting to talk to anybody or do anything." His wife reports that the children are afraid of him. Mike brings his records of his past medical history showing that he "feels like a failure because I've taken everything like I was told and done therapy and none of it has worked." Mike states he "could sleep all day because I can't focus or concentrate." His wife reports that he used to work 60-70 hour weeks and now has started missing work as well as avoiding his friends.

Family History: Dad treated for depression in his 50s after a heart attack.

Medical History: Seizures as an infant, depression for 3+ years, migraine headaches.

Medications: Maxalt for migraines   Substance Use: Coffee 3-4 cups day

What do you do?

Looking over Mike's chart we see the following: Zoloft (sertraline), Celexa (citalopram), Paxil CR (paroxetine), Lexapro (escitalopram) and Prozac (fluoxetine) worked for a little while but had to be increased to higher doses and eventually they all "pooped out." Effexor XR (venlafaxine) at 300 mg had some response but it caused nausea and increased his migraines. Remeron (mirtazapine) had no response even at 60 mg. Because of history of seizures, Mike was not able to take Wellbutrin XL (buproprion).

Diagnosis: Major depressive episode, recurrent

Options

1. Re-evaluate history and symptoms

When patients have multiple antidepressant failures, we need to re-evaluate the symptoms and the working diagnosis and rule out other psychiatric illnesses such as bipolar disorder and ADHD as well as medical conditions that may mimic or exaggerate underlying mood symptoms. Mike has no family history of bipolar, and he and his wife deny any of the symptoms that would point us in that direction. His symptoms are impacting multiple life areas, but he denies suicidal ideation. He recently had a full physical and his PA ruled out cardiovascular problems and thyroid disorder. He describes cognitive difficulty and the desire to "sleep all day" which could be due to excessive daytime sleepiness. Mike and his wife report that he snores very loudly, and occasionally stops breathing during sleep. Mike has been compliant with the medications, and he had some response to SSRIs and NSRIs without prompting a mania.

2. SNRI

While Mike has had a trial with Effexor XR (venlafaxine) with partial response, the side effects stopped him from increasing to the maximum dose. The other medications in this class include Cymbalta (duloxetine), Pristiq (desvenlafaxine) and Savella (milnacipran).

3. Brain Devices

VNS is a new treatment option that received FDA approval in July 2005. The vagus nerve is one of the primary communication pathways from the major organs of the body to the brain. VNS therapy is delivered by a type of pacemaker that sends mild pulses to the vagus nerve in the left side of the neck. VNS therapy targets specific areas of the brain that affect the production or activity of serotonin and norepinephrine. While this treatment is relatively new for treatment resistant depression, a similar treatment has offered remarkable results for epilepsy.

Transcranial magnetic stimulation (TMS) was approved in late 2008 for treatment resistant depression. Brain activity is stimulated by administration of a very strong magnetic field. As you can imagine, insurance providers have been very resistant to paying for these exotic and expensive procedures.

4. Electroconvulsive Therapy (ECT)

Electroconvulsive therapy is the most controversial treatment in psychiatry today. Since Mike's depression has been nonresponsive to therapy and medication interventions, ECT should be considered. It is believed that ECT works through an electrical shock, which causes a seizure to release neurotransmitters in the brain. ECT is clearly indicated when there is an immediate risk of suicide and the depression is incapacitating.

My Choice

Mike needs to know that there is hope in getting him out of this depression. This is the perfect time to review the etiology of depression and help him and his wife see future options clearly. His history strongly suggests Obstructive Sleep Apnea, so referral for further evaluation and treatment becomes a priority, as normalizing his sleep may greatly improve his response to treatment for depression. Since Mike had some response to Effexor XR but stopped due to side effects, we will start Cymbalta at 20 mg daily, increasing by 20 mg weekly. Target dose for Cymbalta is 60 mg but we will monitor response and side effects before increasing at each interval. Many psychiatrists will exceed the recommended dose of Cymbalta if the patient can tolerate it.

Note: If Mike were suicidal and his depression incapacitating, ECT would be a viable next option. There are regional differences in the choice of treatment options for refractory depression. If Mike lived in another part of the world, ECT would be on the top of the treatment list. VNS and TMS are also great ideas, but the cost can be prohibitive.

Likely side effects

Cymbalta: Nausea, dry mouth, constipation, decreased appetite, sedation

Risks

Mike needs to be monitored closely during the first several weeks of treatment. It is rare, but all antidepressants can precipitate suicidal and homicidal ideation.

Resources

Web Sites

Transcranial Magnetic Stimulation
www.mayoclinic.com/health/transcranial-magnetic-stimulation/MY00185

Vagus nerve stimulation
www.vnstherapy.com/depression/whatisvnstherapy/
howvnstherapyworks.asp

ECT
www.psycom.net/depression.central.ect.html

Books

Depression and Bipolar Disorder: Stahl's Essential Psychopharmacology,
3rd edition
Stephen M. Stahl
Cambridge University Press, 2008

Men and Depression: Clinical and Empirical Perspectives (Practical Resources for the Mental Health Professional)
Fredric E. Rabinowitz
Academic Press, 2000

Case of

Paula. Period.

Paula is a 33-year-old married female referred by her physician husband for "mood swings." For several days each month, Paula suffers from insomnia and becomes very irritable, angry, and overwhelmed. She thinks she has adult ADD while her husband wonders if she could be bipolar.

Family History: Mother had postpartum depression requiring hospitalization.

Medical History: Successful in vitro fertilization resulting in a full-term pregnancy three years ago. Migraine headaches since age 14, can be debilitating a few days each month. She complains of significant bloating and breast tenderness before her periods.

Medications: Imitrex (Sumatriptan) as needed for migraines

Substance Use: Three glasses of wine, once or twice monthly.

What do you do?

Paula has symptoms that are suggestive of bipolar disorder. However, with monthly mood symptoms we need to consider menstrual influences. We ask Paula to chart her symptoms for two months using a mood inventory. Reviewing this data, it is clear that Paula only has symptoms before her periods and is fine the rest of the month.

Premenstrual dysphoric disorder (PMDD) affects as many as 5 percent of menstruating women and is characterized by severe mood and physical symptoms around a woman's menstrual cycle, including irritability, tension, low mood and anxiety, and physical symptoms such as bloating and breast tenderness. PMDD symptoms appear 5-10 days prior to menstruation and completely remit when the menstrual cycle begins.

Diagnosis: Premenstrual Dysphoric Disorder (PMDD)

Options

1. No medications—dietary and lifestyle changes

Minimizing caffeine, alcohol and salt intake can help decrease PMDD symptoms. Exercise and stress reduction are important components of a healthy lifestyle. Some women find that vitamin and mineral supplements can also reduce their cyclical symptoms.

2. Antidepressants—SSRI

SSRIs have been successfully used to treat premenstrual mood symptoms for many years. While they all have been found to be helpful in clinical practice only Sarafem (fluoxetine aka Prozac), Paxil CR (paroxetine), and Zoloft (sertraline) are officially approved by the FDA for PMDD.

3. Treat insomnia with a hypnotic

Difficulty sleeping is one of Paula's chief complaints. Any of the available hypnotics may be useful. Tolerance should not be a problem as she would only need the medication for one week each month.

My Choice

Women with premenstrual mood symptoms almost always can benefit from improving their healthy habits: eating properly (minimizing junk food and excess salt intake), eliminating caffeine and alcohol, increasing exercise, calcium supplementation and learning relaxation techniques. However, those with moderate to severe symptoms like Paula often need medication treatment.

Sarafem (fluoxetine) and Zoloft (sertraline) are the first line agents recommended by the American College of Obstetricians and Gynecologists. Many women improve with just a few pills each month. We would begin Paula on fluoxetine 20 mg each month on the day of ovulation. This dose could be increased to 40 and then 60 mg if she still has symptoms. Paxil CR tends to have more weight gain and sexual dysfunction in my experience – I never use it for PMDD.

As needed, hypnotic agents such as Ambien CR, Lunesta or Rozerem may also be beneficial to Paula. We would also suggest couples therapy to deal with marital issues.

Side Effects

SSRIs: Sexual side effects may occur, but are less likely with pulse dosing (brief dosing interval rather than taken every day of the month). Nausea and diarrhea are also possible.

Risks

SSRIs are antidepressants, and the usual precautions should be observed for the emergence of suicidal or homicidal ideation.

Resources

Web Sites

Madison Institute of Medicine
www.pmdd.factsforhealth.org

www.apa.org/monitor/oct02/pmdd.html
Is PMDD real?

www.obgyn.net/women/conditions/pmdd_or_pms.htm
PMDD or PMS—is there a difference?

Menstrual Mood Charting
www.psycheducation.org/FAQ/MoodCharts.htm
A very complete electronic system to chart mood symptoms over time

www.knowmycycle.com

Books

PMDD: A Guide to Coping with Premenstrual Dysphoric Disorder
James E. Huston and Lani Fujitsubo
New Harbinger Publications, 2002

The PMDD Phenomenon: Breakthrough Treatments for Premenstrual Dysphoric Disorder and Extreme Premenstrual Syndrome
Diana L. Dell and Carol Svec
McGraw-Hill, 2002

Dr. Robert Greene's Perfect Balance: Look Younger, Stay Sexy, and Feel Great
by Robert Greene and Leah Feldon
Three Rivers Press, 2006

Peter Pendulum—1

Peter, a 39-year-old divorced male, presents after his former wife urged him to seek treatment. He has had a four-year history of intermittent depressive episodes followed by periods of increased spending (he once bought a Mercedes on his credit card), extramarital affairs, significant insomnia and grandiose thinking.

His wife divorced him earlier in the year because of his behavior.

Family History: Brother has been in jail for embezzlement. Father was an alcoholic who died of liver disease.

Medical History: Asthma   Substance Use: Denies now but drank heavily in college

Medications: Singulair (montelukast) for asthma

What do you do?

This is a classic presentation of bipolar mood disorder. Peter experiences episodes of major depressive disorder followed by manic episodes. We must be sure to consider substance abuse disorders in individuals with these issues. He has a family history of alcoholism and his symptoms could be explained by stimulant abuse (commonly methamphetamine in much of our population). Peter however adamantly denies substance abuse and his urine drug screen is negative for all substances. His family corroborates this history.

Diagnosis: Bipolar I mood disorder

Options

1. No medications—psychotherapy alone

Psychotherapy alone for adults with bipolar disorder is not effective, although psychosocial support is crucial for managing the disorder over the long run. Bipolar disorder is a chronic, recurrent illness that can take a heavy toll on patient and family. Individual and family therapy can help to manage the inevitable problems that arise. Peter signs a consent that allows us to discuss his case with his therapist.

2. Treat with Lithobid or Eskalith (lithium carbonate)

Lithium was the first mood stabilizing medication approved by the FDA. It can be helpful in treating mania and depression as well as preventing future episodes. However, Lithium (despite being a naturally occurring salt) can cause many side effects. It has a narrow window of therapeutic effect, so regular blood levels are necessary.

3. Treat with an anticonvulsant mood stabilizer

Depakote (divalproex sodium) was approved by the FDA as a mood stabilizer in 1995. It is most effective for treating the manic phase and preventing future episodes. It can cause liver problems and blood tests are also required.

Equetro is the brand name of carbamazepine approved by the FDA for bipolar disorder, but other preparations of the same medicine have been used for years. Because there is a rare chance that carbamazepine can cause a blood disorder, blood tests are also required with this medication.

Lamictal (lamotrigine) does not require blood tests. It is particularly helpful for the depressed phase of bipolar disorder.

4. Treat with an antipsychotic mood stabilizer

Zyprexa (olanzapine), Risperdal (risperidone), Seroquel (quetiapine), Abilify (aripiprazole), and Geodon (ziprasidone) are all FDA approved for bipolar disorder. Each has unique benefits and side effects.

My Choice

Treating a newly diagnosed bipolar patient is a challenge. Peter will likely need treatment for a lifetime. There are many different mood stabilizers available and one needs to customize the medication to the patient—not only in terms of efficacy, but side effects. Compliance is often a problem and must be addressed.

Any of the above medicines would be a reasonable choice, but in a young male we would often begin with Zyprexa 20 mg QHS and titrate appropriately.

I strongly recommend mood charting for patients with bipolar disorder.

Likely side effects

Zyprexa is commonly associated with sedation and weight gain

Risks

We warn about weight gain and discuss dietary and behavioral interventions before starting Zyprexa. There also appears to be an increased risk of developing diabetes so we monitor weight, blood pressure, lipids and blood sugars in all patients on antipsychotics.

Bipolar patients may have triple the risk of diabetes over the general public.

Resources

Web Sites

www.manicdepressive.org/images/blankade.pdf
An extensive history form called the Affective Disorders Evaluation, developed by Dr. Gary Sachs

www.manicdepressive.org/images/selfreport.pdf
A checklist designed for patients to complete in between office visits

Mood Charting
www.psycheducation.org/FAQ/MoodCharts.htm
A very complete electronic system to chart mood symptoms over time

Books

Diabetes For Dummies
Alan L. Rubin
For Dummies, 2008

Eat, Drink, and Be Healthy: The Harvard Medical School Guide to Healthy Eating
Walter C. Willett
Free Press, 2005

Eat This, Not That! Thousands of Simple Food Swaps that Can Save You 10, 20, 30 Pounds--or More!
David Zinczenko and Matt Goulding
Rodale Books, 2007

Papers

"Bipolar Disorder and Diabetes Mellitus: Epidemiology, Etiology, and Treatment Implications"
Roger McIntyre, MD et al
Annals of Clinical Psychiatry, 17[2]:83–93, 2005

Weight Gain Liabilities of Common Psychiatric Medications

Antipsychotsics	
Clozapine	Extreme
Zyprexa	Extreme
Risperdal	Moderate
Seroquel	Moderate
Geodon	Mild
Abilify	Mild
Haldol	Mild
Antidepressants	
Remeron	Extreme
Most Tricyclics	Extreme
Paxil	Moderate
Most SSRIs, Effexor XR, Cymbalta	Mild
Wellbutrin	Possible weight loss
Mood Stabilizers	
Depakote	Extreme
Lithium	Moderate
Tegretol	Mild
Lamictal	Mild
Trileptal	Mild
Topamax	Weight loss

Key

Extreme: Weight gain typically 10-20 pounds over a year of treatment

Moderate: Usually not more than 10 pounds over a year

Mild: A few pounds a year, and often no weight gain at all

Case of
Peter Pendulum—2

Remember Peter? Six months ago we started him on Zyprexa for bipolar disorder. He did very well—no more manic or depressive episodes. Unfortunately, he also gained 40 pounds since starting treatment despite exercising four times weekly. Luckily, his blood sugar and lipids are still normal. He now wants to stop his medications as he is now 'better.'

Diagnosis: Bipolar I mood disorder

What would you do now?

Options

1. No medications—psychotherapy alone

Peter still needs medication treatment. Counseling has helped him restore a relationship with his ex-wife and they are now dating again. He realizes that his psychiatric illness has caused much distress among those he loves.

2. Treat with Lithobid or Eskalith (lithium carbonate)

Lithium is still an option. However, it is associated with weight gain.

3. Treat with an anticonvulsant mood stabilizer

Depakote (divalproex sodium) may cause weight gain too.

Equetro (carbamazepine) does not usually cause weight gain.

Lamictal (lamotrigine) does not usually cause weight gain.

Topamax (topiramate) is not approved for bipolar disorder but is sometimes prescribed by psychiatrists to initiate weight loss in patients like Peter.

4. Treat with an antipsychotic mood stabilizer

Risperdal (risperidone) and Seroquel (quetiapine) may cause weight gain, although usually less than Zyprexa. Abilify (aripiprazole) and Geodon (ziprasidone) are much less likely to cause weight gain.

My Choice

The development of intolerable side effects is the most common reason for patients to stop their medications. This is especially important in patients who need to be on long-term treatment. In our experience, Zyprexa is extremely effective but frequently causes unacceptable weight gain.

Upon presenting the options to Peter and he agrees that continuing treatment is the best strategy. He very much dislikes blood tests and consents to a trial of Lamictal because lab monitoring is not necessary.

We begin with 25 mg Lamictal daily, usually in the morning. This is continued for two weeks before increasing to 50 mg qD for another two weeks. We then increase to 75 mg qD for a week or two and then go up to 100 mg qD. Once he is on 100 mg qD, we would begin to gradually decrease his Zyprexa dose until discontinued.

Some patients require further increases up to 300 mg of Lamictal daily.

Likely side effects

Lamictal: Fatigue, dizziness, and rash. Memory impairment at high doses may occur.

Risks

Lamictal is rarely associated with a life-threatening skin rash called Stevens-Johnson Syndrome. The best way to avoid this rash is to introduce Lamictal very slowly. In Peter's case, we would continue the Zyprexa until he reaches an adequate dose of Lamictal.

Resources

Web Sites

www.psycheducation.org/depression/meds/moodstabilizers.htm

www.miminc.org/aboutbipolarinfoctr.asp

Case of

Peter Pendulum—3

Remember Peter? Three months ago we started him on his second medication for bipolar disorder, Lamictal. He was able to slowly discontinue Zyprexa and has lost twenty pounds. A new problem has surfaced: an itchy rash on his chest and back.

Upon seeing the rash, we immediately referred him to a local dermatologist. She biopsied his lesions and confirmed that this was not Stevens-Johnson Syndrome. However, Peter now refuses to continue Lamictal as the rash is uncomfortable.

Diagnosis: Bipolar I mood disorder

What would you do now?

Options

1. No medications—psychotherapy alone

Peter still needs medication treatment. A focus of psychotherapy is now how to live with a chronic illness. He now keeps a log of his medication and its effects, both good and bad. He has read An Unquiet Mind by Kay Jamison. His ex-wife has attended NAMI meetings.

2. Lithobid or Eskalith (lithium carbonate)

Lithium is still an option. However, it is also associated with the possibility of a rash and weight gain. Blood monitoring is required which makes Peter queasy.

3. An anticonvulsant mood stabilizer

Depakote (divalproex sodium) may cause weight gain and requires regular blood monitoring. Equetro (carbamazepine) does not usually cause weight gain but requires blood tests.

4. Atypical antipsychotic mood stabilizer

Weight gain is still a risk with Risperdal (risperidone) and Seroquel (quetiapine). Abilify (aripiprazole) and Geodon (ziprasidone) are unlikely to cause weight gain. Lab monitoring is recommended to follow blood sugars and lipids with all of the medications in this class.

My Choice

We see that every medication has its good and bad effects. Peter has not been able to tolerate Zyprexa nor Lamictal. All of the remaining mood stabilizers require blood tests. We discuss this with Peter's therapist who will begin relaxation training to help him deal with the anxiety of being stuck with a needle.

Peter has seen ads for Equetro and would like to try it. We agree. Start Equetro at 100 mg BID and titrate to efficacy.

Likely side effects

Equetro: Dizziness and drowsiness

Risks

Equetro and Tegretol (both are carbamazepine products) are rarely associated with a decrease in blood cell counts. The name of this problem depends on the severity and the type of blood cells involved. The most extreme example, aplastic anemia, occurs when production of all blood cells stops. This is a medical emergency! If white blood cells called granulocytes are affected, it is called agranulocytosis. If platelets are involved, it is called thrombocytopenia.

We will monitor Peter's CBC—Complete Blood cell Count—regularly to make sure that these problems do not occur. Recommendations vary depending on the source. The Carlat Report (www.thecarlatreport.com) recently reviewed laboratory monitoring in the August 2007 issue. We agree with Carlat's guidelines: baseline—before starting Equetro, one week and one month later, then yearly—as the risk of blood problems is highest in the first month of treatment with carbamazepine.

Case of
Sobbing Sylvia

Sylvia, a 45-year-old homemaker, has been crying "over nothing" for the last several weeks. She also complains of initial insomnia, feeling guilty about her past relationships, trouble concentrating, hopeless feelings and fatigue. She has never felt this way before. She denies any suicidal or homicidal thoughts.

Family History: Grandmother and maternal aunt suffered "breakdowns."

Medical History: Hysterectomy 5 years ago   Medications: None

What do you do?

Sylvia is experiencing her first episode of clinical depression. Although she is reluctant to seek treatment, she feels that her parenting skills are sharply declined and she worries about the negative effect that her mood is having on her children and husband.

Diagnosis: Major depression, single episode

Options

1. No medications—refer for psychotherapy

Cognitive Behavior Therapy (CBT) has been shown to be quite effective in mild to moderate cases of depression. The combination of CBT and antidepressants is the gold standard.

2. Treat with SNRI

Effexor XR (venlafaxine), Pristiq (desvenlafaxine) Cymbalta (duloxetine) are approved for major depressive disorder in adults. They work on both serotonin and norepinephrine. Meta-analyses of depression trials suggest that these agents may help depressed patients get all the way better (or this could be pharmaceutical company hype).

3. Treat with an SSRI

SSRIs such as Prozac (fluoxetine), Zoloft (sertraline), Paxil (paroxetine), Celexa (citalopram) and Lexapro (escitalopram) are commonly used for depressive episodes, especially in primary care settings. They work primarily on serotonin.

4. Treat with a hypnotic

The non-benzodiazepine sleeping agents such as Ambien (zolpidem), Ambien CR, Sonata (zaleplon) and Lunesta (eszopiclone) are approved for sleep initiation. Rozerem (ramelteon) is also approved for sleep onset insomnia and has a novel mechanism of action with no risk of dependence.

5. Treat with sedating antidepressant

Antidepressants such as Remeron (mirtazapine) and Desyrel (trazodone) are quite sedating for many patients and may treat both Sylvia's insomnia and mood.

6. Refer to gynecologist for hormones

Sylvia may be experiencing perimenopausal symptoms. Her ovaries were left intact when her uterus was surgically removed. Without menses as a guide, it can be difficult to determine when estrogen levels drop. Many women who start estrogen replacement therapy find that their mood and sleep patterns improve.

My Choice

Sylvia has classic major depression and may benefit from any of the above treatments. A referral to her to her gynecologist for possible hormone replacement therapy is necessary. Whether to start antidepressants, a sleep aid or psychotherapy (or all three!) can be a difficult decision. Sylvia strongly desires medication treatment because her health insurance does not cover psychotherapy.

Desyrel can be sedating, but we find it to be not terribly effective for depression. Remeron is an extremely effective antidepressant, but its side effects (sedation and appetite increase) can be very unappealing. Effexor XR, Prozac, Pristiq and Cymbalta may exacerbate her insomnia. Zoloft and Lexapro are unlikely to help with sleep problems. Celexa and Paxil are relatively sedating SSRIs that are also available in generic—we would start with Celexa because in our experience it has a more favorable side effect profile. We begin with 10-20 mg QHS and increase if needed.

Likely side effects

All SSRIs can contribute to sexual dysfunction. The problems may be with libido or orgasm or both. Celexa and Paxil can be sedating, which is helpful in the evening but may cause daytime somnolence. In our experience, many patients on SSRIs gain a few pounds over time. A first time SSRI user needs to be watched especially closely for the emergence of suicidal or homicidal thoughts.

Resources

Web Sites

> www.psycom.net/depression.central.html
> Excellent site by Dr. Ivan Goldberg
>
> National Institutes of Mental Health
> www.nlm.nih.gov/medlineplus/hormonereplacementtherapy.html
>
> Massachusetts General Hospital Center for Women's Mental Health
> www.womensmentalhealth.org/topics/mood_auq.html

Books

> *Depression Fallout: The Impact of Depression on Couples and What You Can Do to Preserve the Bond*
> Anne Sheffield
> Quill, 2003
>
> *You Can Think Like a Psychiatrist*
> Leslie Lundt
> Foothills Foundation, 2007
>
> *The Wisdom of Menopause: Creating Physical and Emotional Health and Healing During the Change*, 2nd Edition
> Christiane Northrup
> Bantam, 2006
>
> *A Woman's Guide to Menopause and Perimenopause*
> Mary Rita Minkin and Carol V. Wright
> Yale University Press, 2004
>
> *Menopause Sucks: What to Do When Hot Flashes and Hormones Make You and Everyone Else Miserable*
> by Joanne Kimes
> Adams Media, 2008
>
> *The Secret Pleasures of Menopause*
> Christiane Northrup
> Hay House, 2008

Case of
Wanda Worrywart

Wanda, a 75-year-old widow, has been gradually losing weight over the last two years since the death of her husband. She worries about everything—sometimes calling her children four and five times daily. She is sad and lonely and often tearful. Sleep is not restful; she awakens several times a night. Her bridge group is concerned because she never wants to play cards. She had a similar episode after the birth of her third son.

Family History: None known

Medical History: Hypothyroidism   Substance Use: None

Medications: Synthroid

What do you do?

Wanda's bereavement has progressed into a major depressive episode with recurrent anxious features. She has vegetative symptoms, and her functioning has diminished.

> **Diagnosis: Major depression, recurrent**

Options

1. No medications—refer for psychotherapy

Cognitive Behavior Therapy (CBT) has been shown to be quite effective in mild to moderate cases of depression. Psychotherapy for Wanda would focus on how to live without her husband.

2. Treat with SNRI

Effexor XR (venlafaxine), Pristiq (desvenlafaxine) and Cymbalta (duloxetine) are approved for major depressive disorder in adults. However, they can increase blood pressure.

3. Treat with an SSRI

SSRIs such as Prozac (fluoxetine), Zoloft (sertraline), Paxil (paroxetine), Celexa (citalopram) and Lexapro (escitalopram) are commonly used for elderly depressed patients such as Wanda. Paxil has many potential drug interactions, and side effects such as constipation and should be avoided in the elderly.

4. Treat with a hypnotic

The non-benzodiazepine sleeping agents such as Ambien and Ambien CR (zolpidem), Sonata (zaleplon) and Lunesta (eszopiclone) as well as the newest sleeping agent, Rozerem (ramelteon) are all approved for sleep initiation. Only Lunesta and Ambien CR are approved for sleep maintenance in the elderly.

5. Treat with sedating antidepressant

Antidepressants such as Remeron (mirtazapine) and Desyrel (trazodone) are quite sedating for many patients and may treat both Wanda's insomnia and mood.

6. Refer for dementia workup

It is possible that Wanda's symptoms are early signs of dementia. She certainly needs a complete physical exam and her thyroid functioning tested.

My Choice

Wanda has classic major depression and may benefit from any of the above treatments. Psychotherapy will be an important part of her recovery—she has complicated bereavement and issues regarding possible loss of her independence.

Remeron is an extremely effective antidepressant and often the elderly can benefit from its side effects of sedation and weight gain. It also is available in a generic which may help save her money. This would be our first choice for Wanda. Start Remeron 15 mg nightly then possibly increase up to 45 mg QHS depending on response.

Celexa would be a reasonable choice too. Effexor XR, Pristiq, Prozac and Cymbalta may exacerbate her insomnia and weight loss (because of nausea).

Likely side effects

Remeron can increase appetite which can lead to significant weight gain in some patients. This would be a good thing for Wanda. Sedation is another common problem with Remeron, but we are hoping this will help her sleep more restfully. If daytime sedation persists, we will need to change her antidepressant.

Risks

Wanda is a high suicide risk; she is widowed and feels hopeless. She will need to be monitored closely as antidepressants are started and her mood improves.

Resources

Web Sites

National Institute on Aging publications
www.niapublications.org

Bereavement information
www.nlm.nih.gov/medlineplus/bereavement.html

Information for widows
www.widownet.org

Geriatric Depression Scale
www.stanford.edu/~yesavage/Testing.htm

Books

Grief Expressed When a Mate Dies
Marta Felber
LifeWords, 2008

Widow To Widow: Thoughtful, Practical Ideas For Rebuilding Your Life
Genevieve Davis Ginsburg
Da Capo Press, 2004

Integrated Management of Depression in the Elderly
Carolyn A. Chew-Graham, Robert Baldwin, and Alistair Burns
Cambridge University Press, 2008

Psychotropic Drugs and the Elderly: Fast Facts
Joel Sadavoy
W.W. Norton and Company, 2004

I Wasn't Ready to Say Goodbye Workbook: Surviving, Coping and Healing After the Sudden Death of a Loved One (Workbook)
Brook Noel
Sourcebooks, 2003

Antidepressants (non SSRI)

Relative Adverse Effect Profiles

Agent	Usual Adult Dosage (mg/d)	Drowsiness	Sexual Dysfunction	Agitation/ Insomnia
Ascendin (amoxapine)	200-300	low	high	none
Cymbalta (duloxetine)	20-60	low	moderate	moderate
Desyrel (trazodone)	150-400	very high	none	none
Effexor/Effexor XR (venlafaxine)	75-225	low	high	moderate
Ludiomil (maprotiline)	75-150	moderate	moderate	none
Serzone N/A[*] (nefazodone)	200-600	high	low	none
Remeron SolTab (mirtazapine)	15-45	very high	none	none
Remeron				
Wellbutrin (bupropion)	150-300	none	none	very high
Wellbutrin SR	150-300			
Wellbutrin XL	150-300			
Pristiq (desvenlafaxine)	50	low	moderate	moderate

[*]Serzone is no longer available, but generic nefazodone is.

Adapted from CNS News Special Edition December 2004

Psychotic Disorders

Case of

Psychotic Peggy

Peggy is a 21-year-old woman who has been diagnosed with schizophrenia. Six months ago after weeks of "strange behavior" Peggy was taken by the police to the local psychiatric hospital. She was found walking in the neighborhood at 3 a.m. wrapped in foil with a wire coat hanger wrapped around her head. She reported receiving messages from "the forces" that she had been chosen as the coming Messiah. It has been six months since her hospitalization. Risperdal 4 mg has stopped the voices and allowed her a full night's sleep. At this office visit the voices are at "0" but she says she has missed three periods and her breasts have been leaking "white stuff." Surrounded by support of her family, she "doesn't want to go back to that hell," but has never had these problems before.

Family History: Schizophrenic uncle who committed suicide

Medications: Risperdal 4 mg   Substance Use: 2 PPD cigarettes
Multi-vitamins

Medical History: Negative

What do you do?

Peggy's psychotic break was managed with Risperdal. The negative and positive symptoms of schizophrenia respond well to atypical antipsychotics, however, they are not without side effects which can influence patient compliance.

Peggy is lucky. The symptoms of schizophrenia can permeate every aspect of her and her family's life. She has a supportive family and has successfully stayed on therapy long enough to fully treat her symptoms.

Now what?

When selecting and modifying antipsychotic therapy, we need to incorporate strategies to enhance the quality of life. The level of Risperdal that has proved valuable for treating her symptoms has come with the known adverse event of hyperprolactinemia. High levels of prolactin can cause depression, multiple endocrine disturbances including breast engorgement, disrupted menstruation and if untreated leads to bone demineralization and osteoporosis. These side effects are not just annoying for Peggy; they are threatening her health.

Diagnosis: Schizophrenia

Options

1. Continue Risperdal (risperidone) at lower dose

Increased prolactin levels have been shown to be dose related with Risperdal. She is stable on the 4 mg dose she was started on in the hospital. A possible option would be to decrease the Risperdal and closely monitor her response as well as the impact on her side effects.

2. Switch to Invega (paliperidone ER)

Invega has not received a very warm welcome from psychiatrists even though it is the newest antipsychotic on the market in the US. It is the active metabolite of risperidone which means it is not metabolized in the liver. Daniel Carlat, MD sums up the differences between Invega and Risperdal: "When all is said and done, Invega looks like Risperdal *without* drug-drug interactions, but with *more* QT interval prolongation, *more* tachycardia, *possibly more* EPS, and the same amount of *hyperprolactinemia.*"

3. Switch to other Atypical Antipsychotics

Zyprexa (olanzapine), Seroquel (quetiapine), Geodon (ziprasidone) and Abilify (aripiprazole) have FDA approval for treating positive and negative symptoms of schizophrenia. They all pose low risk of hyperprolactinemia but have different side effect profiles of their own.

4. Rule out tumor on the pituitary gland

The levels of prolactin seen in Risperdal patients are often seen in a pituitary tumor called prolactinoma. Most of the data available about increased prolactin levels have come from research in this area. While pituitary tumors are rare, it is important to rule out anything that might be causing the changes in Peggy's endocrine function.

My Choice

The last thing we want for Peggy is any kind of psychotic decompensation and we need to be vigilant about her quality of life. While trying a lower dose of Risperdal might lower her prolactin levels and stop the side effects it is not worth the risk when there are many other atypical antipsychotics that can keep the positive and negative symptoms at bay. We would cross taper her current medication while starting the new antipsychotic to ensure medication coverage at all times. For one week keep her on Risperdal 4 mg and start Abilify 2.5 mg. Abilify has a mechanism of action that does not increase prolactin levels. We would then taper Risperdal by 0.5 mg each week and increase Abilify by 2.5 mg at weekly office visits to closely monitor the response.

Note Get blood work for prolactin levels at this time to monitor response to taper off Risperdal. Also check fasting glucose, cholesterol and triglycerides because all atypical antipsychotics need monitoring for metabolic changes.

Likely Side Effects

Possible side effects when adding Abilify are headache, anxiety, and insomnia.

Risks

Having two antipsychotic medications on board can increase the risk of neuroleptic syndrome and tardive dyskinesia and can be quite costly.

Resources

Web Sites

National Mental Health Association
www.nmha.org

National Library of Medicine and National Institute of Health
www.nlm.nih.gov/medlineplus/schizophrenia.html

World Fellowship for Schizophrenia and Allied Disorders
www.world-schizophrenia.org

The Carlat Report June 2008 vol 6 number 6
www.thecarlatreport.com

Books

The Complete Family Guide to Schizophrenia: Helping Your Loved One Get the Most Out of Life
Kim T. Mueser and Susan Gingerich
Guilford Press, 2006

Surviving Schizophrenia: A Manual for Families, Patients, and Providers
E. Fuller Torrey
Collins Living, 2006

Getting Your Life Back When You Have Schizophrenia
Robert Temes
New Harbinger Publications, 2008

Case of
Randy's Racket

Randy is a 21-year-old Caucasian male. At the beginning of this past year at college his behavior started to be of great concern to his family and friends. His friends reported that instead of attending classes he was spending his days in his apartment with the blinds closed watching TV. His personal hygiene has deteriorated with his fingernails long and dirty, unshaven, and his hair dirty and matted against his head. His friend contacted his parents, and they immediately moved him out of his apartment and home with them.

He reports hearing voices that argue with each other and states that they prevented him from concentrating on his schoolwork. On questioning, he reports the voices are at a 10 (0 least, 10 most intrusive) and one day in the grocery store they told him to eat only brown cereal and water because everything else is poison. He has lost 50 pounds (weight 120 pounds 5' 10"). While working in the yard over the weekend, Randy told his father the pitchfork and shovel were dangerous weapons and he could not touch them. He is sleeping only 2-3 hours per day, often awake all night watching television or pacing through the house.

Family History: Randy is adopted.

Medications: None

Substance Use: Randy was reporting taking LSD, smoking marijuana, and drinking heavily the 2 months prior to his change of behavior.

What do you do?

Randy's symptoms have impacted every domain in his life. Since there is no family history to show a genetic predisposition for these symptoms, it is important to get history from family and friends who have known Randy for a long time.

> **Diagnosis: Rule out Schizophrenia**
> **Hallucinogen Abuse or Hallucinogen-induced Psychosis**

Options

1. Psychotherapy

Any kind of treatment for people with severe psychotic symptoms is often refused by the patient because they lack insight into their impaired condition. They don't believe they have an illness and see no need for professional intervention particularly when it includes medications or hospitalization. The cognitive impairment inherent to this disorder is likely to limit the degree to which patients can profit from any psychological intervention.

2. Hospitalization

Hospitalization is necessary to treat people with prominent delusions or hallucinations, or serious suicidal thoughts, those who demonstrate an inability to care for themselves, or those with severe problems using drugs or alcohol. It also is important to protect people from hurting themselves or others. Admission to an inpatient psychiatric unit would provide an opportunity for Randy to be closely observed while medications to control his symptoms can be initiated and increased more quickly.

3. Rule out ongoing substance abuse

A thorough history and a urine toxicology screen are needed. Hallucinogens may have long-term effects. A negative toxicology screen does not necessarily mean that Randy's problems are not drug induced.

4. Treat with conventional antipsychotics

Thorazine (chlorpromazine) and Haldol (haloperidol) are medications that were developed decades ago. They can treat the positive psychotic symptoms of schizophrenia, which include hallucinations and delusions. Negative symptoms such as withdrawal, apathy and amotivation are much more resistant to treatment. These medications can cause a wide variety of side effects and have fallen out of favor as first-line choices for psychosis.

5. Treat with atypical antipsychotics

Zyprexa (olanzapine), Risperdal (risperidone), Seroquel (quetiapine), Abilify (aripiprazole) and Geodon (ziprasidone) have shown effectiveness in treating both the positive and negative symptoms of schizophrenia. Each of these medications has its own side effect profile. They can range from weight gain and risk of developing diabetes to sedation and agitation.

My Choice

Randy needs hospitalization immediately. A first psychotic break requires very close supervision and monitoring. The hospital will be a safe place to start medications and titrate the doses faster for symptom relief.

Start Seroquel at 100 mg at night and increase by 100 mg each night aiming for a target dose 600 mg to treat the symptoms of psychosis and to help with sleep. Until the voices are interrupted, his delusions will direct his behavior. Positive symptoms of schizophrenia usually respond quickly to medication.

Is there a reason to use Seroquel XR over Seroquel? The XR formulation is being advertised as more convenient to dose, but I have not found this to be the case.

Side effects

Sedation is the most likely side effect for Randy with Seroquel. Also reported are dizziness, dry mouth and constipation.

Risks

Atypical antipsychotics can predispose Randy to high triglycerides and increased risk for diabetes. Weight, blood sugar and lipid levels need to be monitored regularly.

Resources

Web Sites

www.schizophrenia.com

Practice guidelines

www.psychiatryonline.com/pracGuide/pracGuideTopic_6.aspx

Books

Recovered, Not Cured: A Journey Through Schizophrenia
Richard McLean
Allen and Unwin, 2005

The Day the Voices Stopped: A Schizophrenic's Journey from Madness to Hope
Ken Steele
Basic Books, 2002

I Am Not Sick, I Don't Need Help!
Xavier Amador
Vida Press, 2000

Diagnosis: Schizophrenia
Rachel Miller and Susan Mason
Columbia University Press, 2002

Sleep Disorders

Case of

Coach Camille

Camille is a 33-year-old who is in her first season as a head high school basketball coach and is having trouble getting to sleep on the nights before her games. Running plays and strategies in her head can delay getting to sleep up to two hours. When she doesn't get to sleep at night she often leaves school to go home and take a nap before the game. She has tried over-the-counter sleep aids, but they make her feel hungover the next day. This coaching position is her dream job and this problem is creating doubts that she has what it takes to be successful.

Family History: Dad was also a coach and suffered from pre-game insomnia

Medical History: Tension headaches

Substance Use: Red Bull and occasional wine

Medications: Multivitamins and nutritional supplements

What do you do?

Camille describes her sleep problems as a direct result of ongoing, exciting, yet stressful, events in her life. Initiating sleep is her complaint, but only on nights before games, which creates next day consequences. Otherwise she has no significant anxiety or sleep complaints.

> **Diagnosis: Transient insomnia due to stressful events**

Options

1. No medications—improve sleep hygiene

a. Make sleep a priority with a wind-down time before bed

b. Eliminate alcohol and caffeine

c. Relaxing routine before going to bed—hot bath, reading, music

d. Keep the room dark and cool

e. Finish eating at least three hours before bedtime

f. Aerobic exercise every day, preferably in the morning

2. Psychotherapy for stress management

Therapy is an important tool for stress management. It can be used to explore the roots of thinking and behavior patterns that create unnecessary stress as well as establish realistic goals. Therapy can teach relaxation techniques and break the patterns that are disrupting Camille's sleep.

3. Treat with Rozerem (ramelteon)

Ramelteon is a sleep medication in a class of its own. It works specifically by turning off the brain's wake system and has been shown to be effective in initiating sleep as well as increasing total sleep time.

4. Treat with non-benzodiazepine

Sonata (zaleplon), Ambien (zolpidem), Ambien CR, and Lunesta (eszopiclone) are all FDA approved for insomnia. Sonata has the shortest half-life and is indicated specifically for initiating sleep.

5. Treat with sedating antidepressant

With sedation as one of its major side effects, Desyrel (trazodone) has proven helpful in treating insomnia related to depression and anxiety. The medication can be used as needed for sleep, although research suggests it is not useful in the long-term treatment of insomnia. For some, the hangover, constipation and stuffy nose is not worth the extra sleep.

My Choice

Camille needs psychotherapy to improve her stress management skills. Her father was a coach and she may have adopted some of his tendencies to deal with stress. Therapy will help her identify the patterns that set her up for the anxiety that gets in the way of her sleep.

Improve sleep hygiene. Slowly decrease caffeine intake and eliminate alcohol. Also check ingredients in nutritional supplements as they may contain caffeine or an over-the-counter stimulant. Remind her to begin winding down for sleep an hour before bedtime with soothing rituals (e.g., warm bath, leisure reading), and to turn the clock around so it not visible once she is in bed for the night.

Consider starting Sonata 5-10 mg on nights before a game. Her primary complaint is initiating sleep and Sonata has a rapid onset and short half-life that would allow her to get to sleep and awake refreshed with low risk of next day hangover.

Likely side effects

Stopping caffeine abruptly can lead to withdrawal headaches, so encourage Camille to gradually taper off Red Bull.

Risks

Camille needs to eliminate alcohol on the nights she takes Sonata. Alcohol can decrease sleep quality and quantity, which may worsen her next-day fatigue.

References

Web Sites

www.bettersleep.org
Stress and sleep in America

National Sleep Foundation
www.sleepfoundation.org

Books

The Well-Rested Woman
Janet Kinosian
Conari Press, 2002

A Woman's Guide to Sleep: Guaranteed Solutions for a Good Night's Rest
Joyce A. Walsleben and Rita Baron-Faust
Three Rivers Press, 2001

A Woman's Guide to Sleep Disorders
Meir Kryger
McGraw Hill, 2004

Desperately Seeking Snoozing
John Weidman
Towering Pines Press, 1999

The Insomnia Answer: A Personalized Program for Identifying and Overcoming the Three Types of Insomnia
Paul Glovinsky and Art Spielman
Perigee Trade, 2006

Common Sleep Aids			
Sleep Aid	**Onset of action**	**Elimination half-life**	**Adult dose**
Sonata (zaleplon)	10-20 min	1.0 hrs	5-20mg
Ambien (zolpidem)	10-20 min	1.5-2.4 hrs	5-10mg
Halcion (triazolam)	10-20 min	1.5-5 hrs	0.125-0.25mg
Restoril (temazepam)	45 min	8-20 hrs	7.5-30mg
ProSom (estazolam)	15-30 min	20-30 hrs	0.5-2mg
Dalmane (flurazepam)	15-30 min	36-120 hrs	15-30mg
Xanax (alprazolam)	15-30 min	9-26 hrs	0.25-1mg
Klonopin (clonazepam)	20-60 min	19-50 hrs	0.25-1mg
Lunesta (eszopiclone)	15-30 min	6 hrs	1-3mg
Ambien CR (zolpidem)	10-20 min	2.5 hrs	6.25-12.50mg
Rozerem (ramelteon)	30-90 min	2-5 hrs	8mg

Adapted from CNS News Special Edition December 2004

Case of
Florence Nightingnurse

Florence is a 38-year-old divorced mother of three children who works three 12-hour night shifts on the weekend. She is sent to the clinic by her supervisor because she has fallen asleep while charting several times during the night. She also has had an automobile accident while driving home in the morning after her shift.

Florence states she never had these problems when she worked days or evenings. She often has a headache, is low on energy and has difficulty concentrating. She states she can get to sleep after her shift but wakes up frequently reporting only five or six hours total sleep time. During her days off she has no problem sleeping at night.

Medical History: Negative

Substance use: Florence drinks a triple latte before her shift and 4-5 cups of coffee during her shift. She denies alcohol use.

Medications: Multivitamin

What do you do?

Approximately fifteen million people in the US work at night in medicine, law enforcement, manufacturing, and transportation, to name a few. Since the human body is designed to be awake during the daytime hours and asleep when it is dark, our bodies have a very difficult time adapting to a nighttime work schedule. While changing shifts would be ideal for Florence, due to her family's schedule it is not a viable option.

Diagnosis: Shift Work Sleep Disorder

Options

1. No medications—optimize sleep hygiene behaviors on work days

a. Make sleep a priority every day; minimize daytime interruptions

b. Make the bedroom as dark and quiet as possible

c. Move clocks out of view

d. Keep room at a cool temperature

e. Avoid sunlight on the way home from work by wearing dark sunglasses to delay the wake drive in the circadian system

f. Go directly to sleep at the same time each day

g. Aerobic exercise each day but not near bedtime

h. Limit caffeine intake

Caffeine is most helpful when used only "prn" rather than daily. Tolerance develops quickly to the alerting effects, but the side effects continue. Caffeine also may be causing the headaches that she experiences.

2. Off-label use of stimulants

Ritalin (methylphenidate) and Adderall (D, L amphetamine) have been used to maintain wakefulness during extended duty hours (e.g., the military). The possible side effects of decreased appetite, difficulty sleeping, and tremor can carry over into the rest of her day and night.

3. Provigil (modafinil) and Nuvigil (armodafinil)

Provigil is FDA approved for excessive sleepiness associated with shift work sleep disorder. Provigil has a low side effect profile and while it increases alertness it does not interfere with getting to sleep. The isomer of modafinil, Nuvigil (armodafinil), will be released in mid 2009.

4. Non-benzodiazepine hypnotic

Sonata (zaleplon), Ambien (zolpidem), Ambien CR, and Lunesta (eszopiclone) are hypnotics that have been approved for insomnia. All four have been shown to be effective for initiating sleep.

5. Rozerem (ramelteon)

Rozerem is a non-addicting sleep agent that may be particularly helpful in shift workers because it works to turn off the alerting signal which keeps us awake.

My Choice

Begin with improved self care and sleep hygiene measures. Making sleep a priority includes paying attention to foods and behaviors over the entire 24-hour period. Slowly decrease all caffeine products. Set up a comfortable, desirable place for sleep.

Because of her tremendous sleepiness during work, start Provigil 100 mg and titrate up to 200-400 mg taken at the beginning of her shift. Restoring her alertness is the most important objective, as it is directly correlated with driving safety. The extended wakefulness during her shift will increase her "sleep debt," which, in combination with attention to sleep hygiene, should facilitate 7-8 hours of consolidated sleep. If she continued to have broken sleep after her trial with Provigil and sleep hygiene measures, consider adding Rozerem for sleep initiation.

Likely side effects

Headache is the most common side effect of Provigil which can be minimized by starting with a low dose. The headache can be treated with OTC pain relievers and usually resolves in 2-3 days.

Caffeine withdrawal can also cause headache. This can be avoided by tapering off caffeine slowly.

Risks

Provigil is indicated for the excessive sleepiness related to shift work sleep disorder but should not be used as a substitute for sleep.

Resources

Web Sites

National Sleep Foundation
www.sleepfoundation.org

Sleep Channel: Sleep Community
www.sleepdisorderchannel.net/shiftwork

Department of Labor
Plain Language About Shift Work
www.dol.gov/dol/topic/workhours/nightwork.htm

Shift Work, Circadian Rhythm and Sleep Deprivation Home Page
www.sleepnet.com/shift2000.html

Books

Shift Work: How to Cope: An Introductory Guide
Susan Koen
Round the Clock Resources, 1998

Sleep Secrets for Shiftworkers & People with Offbeat Schedules
David R. Morgan
Whole Person Associates, 1996

The Third Shift: Managing Hard Choices in Our Careers, Homes, and Lives as Women
Michele Bolton
Jossey-Bass, 2000

Caffeine Content

Substance	Caffeine content
Brewed coffee	100mg/6oz
Instant coffee	70mg/6oz
Decaffeinated coffee	4mg/6oz
Tea	40mg/6oz
Caffeine-containing analgesics and cold remedies	25mg/65mg tablet
Stimulants and weight loss aids	75mg/350mg tablet
Starbucks coffee, grande	330mg/16oz
Coca-Cola Classic	35mg/12oz
Mountain Dew	54mg/12oz
Red Bull	76mg/8.3oz
Rockstar	160mg/16oz
NoDoz Maximum Strength	200mg/1 tablet
Hershey's Chocolate Bar	9mg/1.55oz

http://www.mayoclinic.com/health/caffiene/AN01211 (accessed 3.26.2009)

Case of
Jetlag Jerry

Jerry is a 45-year-old senior manager for a computer company who travels to Europe frequently for three or four days at a time. During his stays he experiences grogginess and poor concentration during the day and difficulty getting to sleep at night. He saw an advertisement on television for a sleep aid that isn't "addicting" and wants to try it.

Medical History: Negative

Substance Use: Coffee 2-3 cups each morning, nightly cocktails or wine

Medications: None

What do you do?

Crossing three or more time zones can disrupt sleep cycles and create negative next day consequences. Jerry is responsible for making major business decisions on his trips to Europe and his disrupted sleep schedule is causing problems.

Diagnosis: Transient insomnia due to jet lag

Options

1. No medications—increase sleep hygiene behaviors

a. Start out well rested

b. Drink plenty of water

c. Eliminate caffeine and alcohol

d. Make sleep a priority

e. Get outside in the sunlight everyday, preferably in the early morning

The caffeine and alcohol Jerry is drinking may be compounding his jet lag and his sleep difficulties

2. Non-benzodiazepine hypnotic for sleep

Sonata (zaleplon), Ambien (zolpidem), Ambien CR, Lunesta (eszopiclone) are popular hypnotics. Sonata and Ambien have been approved for short-term treatment of insomnia. Sonata and Ambien both have a short half-life and have shown to help initiate sleep. Lunesta has an indication for both transient and chronic insomnia. Lunesta has a longer half-life and increases total sleep time. Ambien CR can be helpful for sleep onset and sleep maintenance.

3. Off-label use of Provigil (modafinil)

Provigil has been approved for excessive sleepiness related to shift work sleep disorder. It is not approved for the sedation related to jet lag but has a low side effect profile and while it increases alertness it generally does not create problems with getting to sleep when sleep is desired.

4. Melatonin

This naturally secreted hormone has shown some success to help initiate sleep when changing time zones. It is best to begin a few days before traveling east and should be taken at the time sleep will occur in the destination. The dosing can be tricky!

5. Rozerem (ramelteon)

A non-addicting medication that targets the melatonin receptors in the brain has been shown to help initiate sleep.

My Choice

Jerry could benefit from improved sleep hygiene measures. Making sleep a priority includes paying attention to foods and behaviors over the entire 24-hour period. Exposure to sunlight, especially in the morning of the destination, will help shift his schedule. Slowly decrease caffeine intake, limit alcohol, and drink plenty of water. It is also very important that Jerry gets out of his seat during the flight to stretch his legs to minimize the risk of deep vein thrombosis.

Since getting to sleep is Jerry's problem we would start Ambien 10 mg. It has a short half-life and has low incidence of any next day hangover. Ambien needs to be taken specifically before bedtime with the intention of a full night's sleep.

If increasing sleep time does not improve grogginess and poor concentration add Provigil 100-200 mg when Jerry needs to be awake.

Likely side effects

Caffeine withdrawal can cause headaches. A gradual decrease in caffeine will decrease this risk.

Ambien can cause amnesia and hallucinations.

With Provigil, headache is a side effect which can be minimized by titrating to effective dose. The headache can be treated with OTC pain relievers and usually resolves in 2-3 days.

Risks

Provigil has shown to be very useful in treating poor concentration and sleepiness but is not a substitute for sleep.

It is important to instruct patients not to drive while Ambien (or any other hypnotic) is in their system.

Resources

Web Sites

MD Travel Health
www.mdtravelhealth.com/illness/jet_lag.html

www.nojetlag.com

Web MD
www.medicinenet.com/jet_lag/article.htm

Books

How To Beat Jet Lag: A Practical Guide for Air Travelers
Walter Reich, Norman E. Rosenthal, Thomas A. Wehr, Dan A. Oren
Owlet Publishing, 1993

The Cure for Jet Lag
Lynne Waller Scanlon and Charles F. Ehret
Back2Press Books, 2009

Boost Your Vitality With Melatonin: Programming Your Internal Clock For Health & Well-Being
Ingeborg Cernaj
Sterling, 1998

Case of

Sleepless Suzy

Suzy shows up at her doctor's office for her annual physical. She is a 48-year-old CEO. She reports that her periods have been "hit and miss" in the past six months and that she has had a few hot flashes. "I used to sleep like a baby any time and anywhere. Sometimes the problem is getting to sleep and sometimes at 2 a.m. I'm wide awake. Lately I've dreaded bedtime because I don't know what's in store for me. I'm tired all day and can't concentrate enough to function at work. I feel like I'm going crazy."

Family History: Mom died from breast cancer at age 54.

Medical History: Occasional headaches   Medications: Advil or Tylenol

Substance Use: Coffee 2-3 cups day, Wine nightly with dinner

What do you do?

It looks like mid-life (age 48) has put Suzy amidst the predictable symptoms of perimenopause. These symptoms can start 4 to 8 years before full menopause occurs. In addition to changes in a woman's menstrual period, hot flashes, mood disturbances, vaginal dryness, and insomnia can occur. Insomnia can mean having trouble falling asleep, staying asleep and/or feeling like your sleep is not adequate. These nighttime disturbances commonly produce problems the next day, especially difficulty concentrating, irritability, and fatigue. When insomnia occurs on most days for periods lasting more than one month it is said to be "chronic."

Diagnosis: Chronic insomnia, secondary to perimenopause

Options

1. Sleep hygiene

The sixteen hours we spend awake can help set the foundation for the 7-8 hours that we are in bed. Sleep hygiene means identifying behaviors, habits and environmental factors that interfere with sleep. Insomnia treatment always begins with evaluating the above.

a. Avoid heavy meals before bedtime

b. Exercise early in the day

c. Limit or eliminate caffeine and alcohol

d. Create a quiet and consistent routine before getting into bed

e. Make sure the bedroom is cool, quiet and dark

2. Hormone Replacement Therapy (HRT)

Along with reducing hot flashes and night sweats, HRT has helped treat insomnia. The Womens Health Initiative found slightly increased risks of breast cancer and cardiac events with women taking HRT which led many women to abandon their hormones. There is a wide variability of response to HRT and each woman has to weigh the risks and benefits of treating their symptoms.

3. Rozerem (ramelteon)

Rozerem is a selective melatonin receptor agonist and is not to be confused with over-the-counter melatonin found in health food stores. Melatonin receptors in the brain are involved in the maintenance of the circadian rhythm underlying the normal sleep-wake cycle. Rozerem has been shown to shorten the amount of time it takes to get to sleep.

4. Non-benzodiazepines

Ambien CR (zolpidem) and Lunesta (eszopiclone) are approved for getting people to sleep and keeping them asleep. Because they are specific to the part of the brain that initiates sleep and have a short half-life, they have a low incidence of side effects and next day consequences.

5. Off-label medications

Neurontin (gabapentin) has been demonstrated to improve sleep continuity in perimenopausal women experiencing hot flashes. Effective doses range from 200-900 mg nightly. Many antidepressants have been helpful in reducing hot flashes, but Effexor XR and Paxil are most commonly used.

My Choice

We will start Lunesta 3 mg immediately. Lunesta is FDA approved for the long-term treatment of both sleep onset and sleep maintenance insomnia. Lunesta should help her get to sleep and keep her asleep so she can have the energy, focus and concentration that she needs to function. While Lunesta will treat the insomnia symptoms, it will not treat her hot flashes and missed periods. However, in a published study, Lunesta was shown to decrease the number of awakenings due to hot flashes. Due to her family history of breast cancer, she may not be a candidate for HRT. She will need to work closely with her health care provider to treat those symptoms in other ways.

Suzy holds a high stress position and needs to create a balance for work and the rest of her life and make sleep a priority. Until she establishes a good night's sleep, switch to decaffeinated drinks and limit nightly wine with dinner.

Likely side effects

Caffeine withdrawal can cause headache. A gradual decrease in caffeine is advised. Lunesta often creates an unpleasant taste in the mouth. Minimize this by drinking orange juice in the evening with the medication.

Risks

Lunesta should be taken only when Suzy is able to go directly to bed for a full night's sleep.

Resources

Web Sites

> Alexander Foundation for Women's Health
> www.afwh.org
> Information on menopause, mood and quality of life. Terrific free podcasts!

> The National Sleep Foundation
> www.sleepfoundation.org

> The Hormone Foundation, an Affiliate of the Endocrine Society
> www.hormone.org

> The North American Menopause Society
> www.menopause.org

Books

> *The Wisdom of Menopause*
> Christiane Northrup
> Bantam, 2006

> *A Woman's Guide to Menopause and Perimenopause*
> Mary Jane Minkin and Carol Wright
> Yale University Press, 2004

> *The Woman's Book of Sleep: A Complete Resource Guide*
> Amy R. Wolfson and Kathyrn A. Lee
> New Harbinger Publications, 2001

> *A Woman's Guide to Sleep Disorders*
> Meir H. Kryger
> McGraw-Hill, 2004

> *A Woman's Guide to Sleep: Guaranteed Solutions for a Good Night's Rest*
> Joyce A. Walsleben and Rita Baron-Faust
> Three Rivers Press, 2001

Sleep Diary							
	Mon	**Tue**	**Wed**	**Thu**	**Fri**	**Sat**	**Sun**
Sleep Patterns							
Time I went to bed							
Time I woke up							
Time it took me to fall asleep							
Number of times I woke up during the night							
Number of minutes I was awake during the night							
I felt refreshed when I woke up (Y/N)							
Daytime Activities							
Total time I napped							
Time I exercised							
There was a stressful event in my day (Y/N)							
Number of alcoholic drinks I consumed							
Number of caffeinated drinks I consumed							
During the day, I feel— 1- very tired 2- somewhat tired 3- normal 4- wide awake							

Case of

Nigel Nightowl

It is early August. Nigel, a 16-year-old high school junior, is brought reluctantly to the clinic by his mother. Mom complains that "in the last three years he has become lazy, unmotivated, and falls asleep in class." Nigel fell asleep in the car on the way to the 9 a.m. visit and had to be awakened in the waiting room. Nigel barely passed his classes last year with C's. He is on a first name basis with everyone in the principal's office because he has been in detention for falling asleep in class. "I'm never tired before 2 or 3 a.m. and all my friends are up at that time." Nigel's first period starts at 7:30 a.m. and his mom sets three alarm clocks to wake him up. He drinks a large Starbucks coffee on the way to school and still falls asleep in his classes. He says he wakes up after 3 p.m. and is able to "kick butt" with his friends on computer games all night long. If left to his desired schedule, he says he would go to bed at 3 a.m. and wake up at noon.

Mom is determined she will not go through another year this way.

Family History: Father is a "night owl"

Medical History: Negative

Medications: None   Substance Use: Caffeine 3-4 times a day

What do you do?

Nigel is getting good sleep—just at the wrong time. The "darkness hormone," melatonin, increases at night and helps us fall asleep. Adults start to produce melatonin around 9 p.m. and are able to fall asleep shortly after that time. Teenagers studied in a sleep lab showed that they begin to increase melatonin at 1 a.m., which explains why they have no desire to turn out the lights at the same time as their parents, and can't fall asleep even when they do! Their brains are still awake, and their circadian rhythm hasn't okayed the transition to sleep. Some people are natural night owls, and during the teen years their circadian rhythm is further delayed. Following their brain's preferred schedule becomes a huge problem when school starts at 7:30 a.m.

Diagnosis: Circadian rhythm disorder, Delayed Phase Sleep Disorder (DPSD)

Options

1. Working with the school system

Starting school at 7 a.m. or an early sports practice is setting Nigel up for failure unless he is highly motivated. Mom needs to advocate for him to start classes later and stay after school independently to make up his work. "Detention" for responding to his biological drive takes a shot at Nigel's self esteem. Sleepiness impacts his attention and memory, and this decreases learning.

2. Chronotherapy

Chronotherapy involves going to sleep 1 to 2 hours later every 2-3 days until you go around the clock and reach the desired bedtime. Chronotherapy is difficult, although for teens with DSPS it is much easier than going "cold turkey" and waking up at 6 a.m. on the first day. The difficult part for the teen is the need to be rigid about the sleep/wake schedule. Once the schedule is established, only an extra 30 minutes on the weekend can be added.

3. Phototherapy

Light exposure in the morning advances the sleep phase and light in the evening delays it. No teen with DSPS has the time to sit in front of a light box for 30 minutes in the morning when they are squeezing every minute they can into sleep. A "dawn simulator" sets the lights to come on about an hour before Nigel wakes up. On the other end of the day, lights need to be dim by 9 p.m. with no computer or television light stimulation. Good luck!

4. Melatonin

Melatonin is a hormone secreted by the pineal gland that helps decrease the brain's alerting mechanism. It must be taken 3-4 hours before the desired sleep time and can help initiate sleep. There is no FDA approval for this therapy, and melatonin can be purchased in health food stores. Because it is not considered a medicine, melatonin is not regulated and is notoriously inconsistent from bottle to bottle.

5. Eliminate caffeine

Nigel is using caffeine in high doses and it is not working to wake him up. If caffeine is used occasionally rather than daily it has more impact on the alerting part of the brain. Tolerance develops quickly to the alerting effects but the sleep interruption side effects continue.

My Choice

In addition to mom getting support from the school system, Nigel needs to be 100% invested in this process. It will not be easy for him to change the social expectations. Since it is the first of August there is time to establish a new sleep schedule through chronotherapy. Get Nigel into sunlight early every day and invest in a light box for the shorter days and no video games or television an hour before going to bed. It will be important for Nigel to decrease his caffeine intake as well as get exercise on a daily basis. It is reasonable to try melatonin 1-2 mg 3-4 hours before sleep time until sleep schedule is reset.

Likely side effects

Caffeine withdrawal can bring headaches. Suggest a slow taper to minimize the risk.

Risks

Melatonin can create sedation and should only be taken when a full night's sleep is expected. Melatonin also can provoke vivid, uncomfortable dreams. Stick with the same brand to minimize inconsistencies.

Resources

Web site

National Sleep Foundation
www.sleepfoundation.org
Adolescent sleep needs and patterns

Light Therapy Products
www.lighttherapyproducts.com
Products available for treating patients with light

National Institutes of Health ("Awake at the Wheel")
www.nhlbi.nih.gov/health/public/sleep/aaw/brochure.pdf
Brochure to download

http://kidshealth.org/teen/your_body/take_care/sleep.html

Mayo Clinic ("Adolescent Sleep Problems: Why Is Your Teen So Tired?")
www.mayoclinic.com/health/teens-health/CC00019.com

Books

Yes, Your Teen Is Crazy! Loving Your Kid without Losing Your Mind
Michael J. Bradley
Harbor Press, 2003

Dead on their Feet: Teen Sleep Deprivation and its Consequences
Joan Esherick
Mason Crest Publishing, 2004

A Clinical Guide to Sleep Disorders in Children and Adolescents
Gregory Stores
Cambridge University Press, 2001

Take Charge of Your Child's Sleep: The All-in-One Resource for Solving Sleep Problems in Kids and Teens
by Judith A. Owens and Jodi A. Mindell
Da Capo Press, 2005

The Body Clock Guide to Better Health : How to Use Your Body's Natural Clock to Fight Illness and Achieve Maximum Health Michael
Smolensky and Lynne Lamberg
Holt Paperbacks, 2001

Case of

Warren A. Widower

Warren is a 75-year-old farmer whose wife, Ida, died six months ago after a struggle with cancer. He reports times when he is very sad and "I miss her badly but I have 55 years of memories to draw from." He reports that farming and taking care of his animals and crops have helped keep his spirits up. Long time friends and his family call on him daily. Since his wife died he has had trouble getting to sleep. "If I can just get to sleep I'm good for the night. It just seems strange climbing into that bed alone after all these years. I have started taking naps, and that is not like me. I turn the TV on when I can't sleep and I've seen advertisements for sleep medications. I hear they are not addicting and I want to try one."

Medical History: Hypertension and arthritis. Weight is within normal limits, denies snoring.

Medications: Lopressor 50 mg, Excedrin as needed for arthritis pain.

Substance Use: Coffee 2 cups in the morning. Warren has been in recovery for alcoholism and opiate abuse since returning from the Korean War. Active in AA.

What do you do?

Problems with sleep occur in over half of adults age 65 and older. While the need for sleep doesn't change as we age, there are many interruptions for the elderly that can eat into sleep quality. Older people do best on seven to eight hours of sleep a night, just like everybody else. Warren is experiencing symptoms of insomnia that are directly related to a major change in his life.

Diagnosis: Chronic insomnia

Options

1. Improve Sleep Hygiene

Treating insomnia starts by looking at the behaviors, habits and environment that can interfere with a good night's sleep. Warren's arthritis might cause pain that would interfere with his sleep so that needs to be addressed. His farming takes him outside working in the fields and taking care of his animals. That adds exercise and sunlight which are both positive forces to help with sleep.

a. Limit or eliminate caffeine

b. Set a consistent bedtime and stick with it

c. Make sure bedroom is dark, cool and quiet

d. Avoid napping more than half an hour during the day

e. Avoid eating anything but a light snack before bedtime

3. Psychotherapy

The loss of a spouse is a very stressful time for the elderly and brings tremendous grief. This needs to be acknowledged because their world is changing, and often shrinking at the same time. Therapy can help identify problems the husband might have in separating from his wife. Group therapy can be valuable to connect with others who have had a similar experience.

4. Non-benzodiazepine hypnotics

Sonata (zaleplon), Ambien, Ambien CR (zolpidem) and Lunesta (eszopiclone) are short-acting hypnotics that have been approved for insomnia. All four have been shown effective for initiating sleep and Ambien CR and Lunesta increase total sleep time.

5. Rozerem (ramelteon)

Rozerem was given FDA approval in July 2005 for treating patients who have a difficult time getting to sleep and has been studied in patients up to 93 years old. It is described as a melatonin (MT1 and MT2) receptor agonist and acts specifically on these two receptors located in an area of the brain called the suprachiasmatic nucleus (SCN) also referred to as the body's "master clock". Rozerem is not a controlled substance and, as such, has no risk of abuse or dependence.

My Choice

Since getting to sleep is Warren's major complaint, we will start him on Rozerem 8 mg. He needs to take it within 30 minutes of heading to bed. It is also recommended that Rozerem not be taken with or immediately after a high fat meal. It might not hurt to have Warren drink decaffeinated coffee until his sleep is restored.

It has been only six months since Warren's wife died so he is still in the early stages of grief. He is lucky to have friends and family nearby but he may also benefit from a grief group in his faith community or through the local senior center. We will follow up with him weekly for the first month to check progress on both his sleep and how he is coping with this loss. Be on the lookout for increased depressive symptoms and suicidal ideation.

Likely side effects

Rozerem: somnolence, fatigue, dizziness

Risks

Take Rozerem only when you know you are headed to sleep.

Resources

Web Sites

    www.4therapy.com
    Therapy Network

    American Association of Retired Persons
    www.aarp.org

    National Institute of Aging
    www.nia.nih.org

    National Sleep Foundation
    www.sleepfoundation.org

    Sleeping Pills, New and Old
    The Carlat Report volume 5 number 2 December 2007
    www.thecarlatreport.com

Books

    The Gentle Closings Companion: Questions And Answers For Coping With The Death Of Someone You Love
    Ted Menten
    Running Press, 2002

    The Light at the End of the Tunnel: Coming Back to Life After a Spouse Dies
    Mary Menke
    AuthorHouse, 2006

    The Death of a Wife: Reflections for a Grieving Husband
    Robert Vogt
    ACTA Publications, 1997

Substance Abuse Disorders

Al Kohall

Al Kohall, a 55-year-old married male, presents with his wife after he has finished an outpatient alcohol treatment program.

He admits to a 35-year history of increasing alcohol intake. A second DUI arrest three months ago prompted his admission into treatment. He has done quite well in the program and has fully embraced AA, attending daily meetings. Since detox, he has had difficulty falling and staying asleep, intermittent anxiety, and an intense craving for alcohol. His temporary sponsor is concerned that his continued discomfort will lead to relapse.

Family History: Father died of cirrhosis of the liver. Brother is an IV drug addict.

Medical History: Acid reflux

Other substance use: Smokes 2 PPD

Medications: Prilosec (omeprazole)

What do you do?

Deciding whether or not to use psychotropic medications in patients with a history of substance abuse or dependence is one of the most difficult decisions we must make. Not treating Al Kohall may lead to his returning to alcohol to medicate his distress. Treating him with potentially addicting medications may also hasten relapse or lead to prescription drug dependence.

Diagnosis: Alcohol dependence with physiological dependence

Options

1. No medications—12 Step and group therapy alone

Certainly continuation in AA and follow up in his aftercare group is critical for Al. The question becomes, is AA enough in someone with post-acute withdrawal symptoms? If alcoholism is a disease, why are we so reluctant to use medicines to treat that disease?

2. Treat with hypnotic

Al Kohall has initial and middle insomnia—one could argue to treat his sleep problems first. However, most of the current FDA-approved medications for insomnia are all potentially abusable. The mechanism of action of benzodiazepines such as Restoril (temazepam) as well as non-benzo hypnotics such as Ambien (zolpidem) involve GABA—just like alcohol. Most addiction professionals strongly discourage prescribing medications similar to a patient's drug of choice. Rozerem (ramelteon) is a new non-addicting sleep agent that is beneficial in treating substance abusers.

3. Treat with anti-anxiety agents

Anxiety is often a significant symptom of post-acute alcohol withdrawal. As above, benzodiazepines such as Xanax (alprazolam) or Klonopin (clonazepam) are generally not recommended treatments in this population. A non-addicting alternative would be BusPar, which works via serotonin. Antidepressants such as an SSRI or Effexor XR could also help his symptoms. Desyrel (trazodone) may be useful for its mild antianxiety effects and its sedation when taken at night for sleep.

4. Use Antabuse (disulfiram)

Antabuse has been available for 50 years. It works to interfere with the metabolism of alcohol so that if someone drinks while taking this medication, he can become very ill. Antabuse is an aversive treatment and will not help his protracted withdrawal symptoms.

5. Use ReVia (naltrexone)

ReVia blocks opiate receptors and may decrease craving by decreasing the pleasure associated with alcohol. A long-acting injectable version, Vivitrol can enhance compliance.

6. Use Campral (acamprosate)

Campral has been introduced in the US after being available in Europe for many years. It works by calming the glutamate system and should help with craving and symptoms of protracted withdrawal.

My Choice

A combination of Campral and naltrexone (either oral or depot injection) is the best bet. Craving is attacked both from the pleasure and withdrawal end. We try to avoid benzos and hypnotics in alcoholics, but Rozerem is a good option if insomnia persists. The sexual side effects of antidepressants make compliance an issue. BusPar is a reasonable alternative, but may take weeks to work and the benefits, if any, are often mild. It must be emphasized that the overall treatment plan is most effective when pharmacology is used as an adjunct with a combination of 12-step recovery programs, and individual and family therapy.

Likely side effects

Campral—diarrhea, nausea and headache.

Risks

Medication alone rarely works in substance abusers.

Resources

Web Sites

National Institute on Alcohol Abuse and Alcoholism
www.niaaa.nih.gov

Alcoholics Anonymous
www.aa.org

National Clearinghouse for alcohol and Drug information
www.health.org

Campral (acamprosate) information
www.fda.gov/cder/consumerinfo/druginfo/Campral.htm

ReVia (naltrexone) information
www.well.com/user/woa/revia/reviafaq.htm

www.chce.research.va.gov/apps/PAWS/

Books

A Primer of Drug Action: A Concise, Nontechnical Guide to the Actions, Uses, and Side Effects of Psychoactive Drugs
Robert M. Julien
Worth Publishing, 2001

Clinical Manual Of Addiction Psychopharmacology
Henry R. Kranzler and Domenic Ciraulo
American Psychiatric Publishing, 2005

Treating Alcohol and Drug Problems in Psychotherapy Practice: Doing What Works
by Arnold M. Washton and Joan E. Zweben
Guilford Press, 2008

Medications to try for Alcoholism

Medication	Mechanism	Dosage	Notes
ReVia (naltrexone)	Opiate blocker	50mg qD	Recent large VA study was negative
Vivitrol (naltrexone depot)	Opiate receptor blocker	380mg Q 28 Days	Injectable
Campral (acamprosate)	Modulates Glutamate	666mg TID	Has been used in millions of patients
Zofran (ondansetron)	$5HT_3$ Blocker	0.5mg qD	Effective for early-onset alcoholics in early data
Topamax (topiramate)	Stimulates GABA	150mg BID (titrate slowly)	Limited data but looks promising

Adapted from The Carlat Report on Psychiatric Treatment (www.TheCarlatReport.com) 2004, Volume 2, Number 3. Copyright © Clearview Publishing 2004. Used with permission.

Case of

Nick Nicotine

Nick Nicotine, a 39-year-old carpenter, presents because his uncle was just diagnosed with lung cancer. He says that he is now motivated to "really quit this time". He has been smoking two packs of filtered cigarettes daily since his teens. In the past he has stopped for as long as three weeks, but always resumes his habit.

Family History: Father, brother, three uncles are all heavy smokers. Wife quit cold turkey three years ago and cannot understand why Nick is "so weak."

Mother has been on unknown antidepressant for years.

Medical History: Environmental allergies

Substance Use: 2 PPD cigarettes + 3 beers weekly

Medications: Claritin (loratadine) as needed for allergies

What do you do?

Nick is now highly motivated to quit smoking. As he has been unsuccessful in the past, medical intervention is warranted. Nicotine is a highly addictive drug and may require detoxification. The most important life-saving intervention in any practice is to help patients stop smoking.

Diagnosis: Nicotine dependence

Options

1. No medications—refer for cognitive behavior therapy, hypnotherapy, biofeedback, or acupuncture.

Smokers can often benefit from these modalities. However, Nick has a strong physical addiction to nicotine that needs to be addressed.

2. Treat with nicotine replacement

Nicotine replacement was the first pharmacologic therapy to be approved by the FDA for smoking cessation. There are many forms now available: gum (Nicorette), transdermal patch (NicoDerm, Nicotrol), inhaler (Nicorette), lozenge (Commit), and spray (Nicotrol NS). The idea behind nicotine replacement is to treat the withdrawal syndrome that occurs when smoking is stopped. The nicotine dose is gradually decreased,

140

minimizing discomfort. This option is for patients who are physically addicted to nicotine.

3. Treat with Zyban

Zyban is bupropion—the same medicine as Wellbutrin SR. Although it is an antidepressant, studies show that Zyban can be helpful in smokers who are not depressed. Unlike nicotine replacement, Zyban works to change brain chemistry to reduce craving for nicotine. It is believed to work by increasing available dopamine in the centers of the brain that control reward.

4. Treat with Chantix (varenicline)

Chantix is a partial nicotine agonist that attempts a delicate balancing act of stimulating brain nicotine receptors just enough to eliminate the reward from smoking and prevent withdrawal symptoms, but not so much that the drug itself is addictive.

My Choice

Nick needs a team approach if he is to become a non-smoker. We recommend behavioral therapy, support groups, and Chantix. Chantix needs to be started while he is still smoking. After one to two weeks on the medicine, he then picks a date to stop smoking. We have had amazing results with this approach but patients need to stay on the medicine for at least 12 weeks to avoid relapse.

Likely side effects

Chantix commonly causes nausea and bizarre dreams. We try to minimize the nausea by slowly titrating the dose and giving the medicine with food and a full glass of water.

Risks

Chantix is rarely associated with psychiatric symptoms such as changes in behavior, agitation, depressed mood and suicidal ideation. Discuss this with Nick prior to beginning treatment.

Zyban is an antidepressant and is associated with a very low risk of increased suicidal or homicidal ideation. It should not be used in patients with seizure disorders.

Resources

Web Sites

QuitNet
www.quitnet.com
A terrific resource for patients who are ready to quit (includes search of local programs in your area)

University of California, San Francisco
www.stopsmoking.ucsf.edu
A free Web-based smoking cessation course

The Foundation for a Smoke-Free America
www.anti-smoking.org

Books

Complete Idiot's Guide to Quitting Smoking
Lowell and Deborah Kleinman
Alpha, 2000

The Easy Way to Stop Smoking: Join the Millions Who Have Become Non-Smokers Using Allen Carr's Easyway Method
Allen Carr
Sterling, 2005

American Lung Association
7 Steps to a Smoke-Free Life
Edwin B. Fisher
Wiley, 1998

Manual of Smoking Cessation: A Guide for Counselors and Practitioners
Andy McEwen, Peter Hajek, Hayden McRobbie, and Robert West
Wiley-Blackwell, 2006

Cognitive-Behavioral Therapy for Smoking Cessation: A Practical Guidebook to the Most Effective Treatments
Kenneth A. Perkins, Cynthia A. Conklin, and Michele D. Levine
Routledge, 2007

Comparison of Nicotine Replacement Products

NRT Form	Availability	Flexible Dosing	Min/Max Dose	Time To Onset	Oral Delivery	Primary Side Effects
Nicotine Patch	Over-the-Counter	Yes	1 daily	1-3 hours	No	topical skin rash
Nicotine Gum	Over-the-Counter	Yes	9-20 daily	7-10 mins	Yes	mouth/throat soreness
Nicotine Lozenge	Over-the-Counter	Yes	9-20 daily	7-10 mins	Yes	hiccups; heartburn
Nicotine Inhaler	Prescription	Yes	6-16 daily	5 mins	Yes	cough; throat irritation
Nasal Spray	Prescription	Yes	13-20 daily	10-15 mins	No	nose/throat irritation; runny nose

(Adapted from Schmitz J., Henningfield J, Jarvik M, "Pharmacologic Therapies for Nicotine Dependence." In Principles for Addiction Medicine, 2nd ed., 1998). From www.quitnet.com/library/guides/NRT/NRT_chart.jtml

Reviewers

Susan Farber PhD
Gordon Robinson MD
Patricia Paddison MD
Antonia Baum MD
Charles Price MD
Kai McDonald MD
Mary O'Malley MD, PhD
Jonathan Schwartz MD
Warner Schwarner MD
John Schmitz MD
James Hancey PhD, MD
Roger McIntyre MD
Cynthia Brownsmith PhD
Jo Frederic MSW
Sandeep Kapoor MD
Abraham Kryger MD
Ruth Goldfinger Golomb
H. Brent Solvason MD, PhD
Lane Cook MD
Steve Soldinger MD
Terry Ribbens MD

Pierre Blier MD
Marty Gabica MD
Barbara Miller NP
Paula Hensley MD
Jeremy Cole MD
Jeffrey Berlant MD, PhD
Joseph Murphy PA
H. George Nurnberg MD
Justine Petrie MD
Millie Smith MEd
Diane M Kendall APRN, MS, FNP
Cheryle Jones Andrews LPCP
Susan Reuling Furness LPCP
Sallye Stauber FNP, MSN
Lou Mini, MD
Rob Rubens, MD, MBA
Carey Crill, ARNP
Ovidio Bermudez, MD
Michael Kalm, MD
Scott Armentrout, PhD

I learned much from colleague reviewers, but didn't always agree with them! If you describe the same patient to six clinicians, you will likely obtain six different treatment regimens. Medicine is still largely an art.

Abbreviations and Acronyms

ACE	angiotensin converting enzyme
ADHD	attention deficit hyperactivity disorder
BID	twice a day
BUN	blood urea nitrogen
CBC	complete blood count
CBT	cognitive behavior therapy
CD	controlled delivery
CR	controlled release
ECT	electroconvulsive therapy
EKG	electrocardiogram
FDA	Federal Drug Administration
GAD	generalized anxiety disorder
GI	gastrointestinal
LA	long-acting
LFT	liver function tests
MAO	monoamine oxidase
NMDA	N-methyl-D-aspartic acid
NRP	nicotine replacement products
NSRI	norepinephrine serotonin reuptake inhibitor
OCD	obsessive compulsive disorder
PPD	packs per day
PRN	take as needed
PTSD	post traumatic stress disorder
PMDD	premenstrual dysphoric disorder
q AM	every morning
qD	every day
QTc	an EKG interval
SNRI	serotonin norepinephrine reuptake inhibitor
SSRI	selective serotonin reuptake inhibitor
TCA	tricyclic antidepressants
TCR	The Carlat Report
TSH	thyroid stimulating hormone
VNS	vagus nerve stimulation
XL	extended length
XR	extended release

Index of drugs: brand and generic names

A

Abilify (aripiprazole) 56, 66, 70, 79, 91, 94, 96, 107, 110

acamprosate. See Campral

Acomplia (rimonabant) 141

Adderall (amphetamine) 118

alprazolam. See Xanax

Ambien (zolpidem) 73, 99, 102, 114, 116, 118, 121, 125, 133, 137

amphetamine. See Adderall

Anafranil (clomipramine) 14, 17, 48

Antabuse (disulfiram) 137

Aricept (donepezil) 43, 45

aripiprazole. See Abilify

Ascendin (amoxapine) 104

atenolol. See Tenormin

Ativan (lorazepam) 5

atomoxetine. See Strattera

B

bupropion. See Wellbutrin

bupropion. See Zyban

BusPar (buspirone hydrochloride) 6, 7, 14, 25, 137

C

Campral (acamprosate) 66, 137, 138, 139

Captopril (ACE inhibitor) 72

carbamazepine. See Equetro

Celexa (citalopram) 3, 10, 60, 63, 84, 98, 101

chlordiazepoxide. See Librium

citalopram. See Celexa

clomipramine. See Anafranil

clonazepam. See Klonopin

clorazepate. See Tranxene

Cognex (tacrine) 45

Cymbalta (duloxetine) 60, 63, 73, 76, 85, 98, 101, 104

D

Dalmane (flurazepam) 116

Depakote (divalproex sodium) 56, 66, 70, 78, 91, 94, 96

desipramine. See Norpramin

Desoxyn (methamphetamine) 23

Desyrel (trazodone) 20, 99, 102, 104, 137

Dextrostat (D-amphetamine) 28

diazepam. See Valium

disulfiram. See Antabuse

donepezil. See Aricept

duloxetine. See Cymbalta

E

Effexor (venlafaxine) 60, 63, 73, 76, 84, 85, 98, 101, 104

Equetro (carbamazepine) 56, 66, 70, 78, 91, 94, 96 escitalopram. See Lexapro

Eskalith (lithium carbonate) 90, 94, 96

eszopiclone. See Lunesta

Exelon (rivastigmine) 43, 45

F

fluoxetine. See Prozac

flurazepam. See Dalmane

fluvoxamine. See Luvox

G

galantamine. See Razadyne

Geodon (ziprasidone) 56, 66, 70, 79, 91, 94, 96, 107, 110

H

Halcion (triazolam) 116

Haldol (haloperidol) 42, 110

haloperidol. See Haldol

I

imipramine. See Tofranil

Inderal (propranolol) 3

K

Klonopin (clonazepam) 3, 5, 20, 116, 137

L

Lamictal (lamotrigine) 66, 70, 78, 91, 94

lamotrigine. See Lamictal

Lexapro (escitalopram) 3, 10, 51, 60, 63, 84, 98, 101

Librium (chlordiazepoxide) 5

lithium carbonate. See Eskalith

lorazepam. See Ativan

Ludiomil (maprotiline) 104

Lunesta (eszopiclone) 73, 99, 102, 114, 116, 118, 121, 125, 133

Luvox (fluvoxamine) 3, 10, 14, 16, 48

M

maprotiline

memantine. See Namenda

methamphetamine. See Desoxyn

methylphenidate. See Ritalin

mirtazapine. See Remeron

modafinil. See Sparlon and Provigil

N

naltrexone. See ReVia

Namenda (memantine) 43, 45

Nardil (phenelzine) 10

nefazodone. See Serzone

Neurontin (gabapentin) 125

Norpramin (desipramine) 10

O

olanzapine. See Zyprexa

oxazepam. See Serax

P

Parnate (tranylcypromine) 10

paroxetine. See Paxil

Paxil (paroxetine) 3, 10, 19, 60, 63, 84, 98, 101

phenelzine. See Nardil

propranolol. See Inderal

ProSom (estazolam) 116

Provigil (modafinil) 23, 118, 122

Prozac (fluoxetine) 3, 10, 16, 48, 51, 60, 63, 75, 84, 98, 101

Q

quetiapine. See Seroquel

R

ramelteon. See Rozerem

Razadyne (galantamine) 43, 45

Remeron (mirtazapine) 33, 84, 99, 102

Remeron SolTab (mirtazapine) 104

Restoril (temazepam) 116, 137

ReVia (naltrexone) 137, 138, 139 rimonabant. See Acomplia

Risperdal (risperidone) 56, 66, 70, 79, 91, 94, 96, 110

risperidone. See Rispderdal
Ritalin (methylphenidate) 27, 118
rivastigmine. See Exelon
Rozerem (ramelteon) 102, 114,
    116, 118, 122, 125, 133, 137

S

Sarafem (fluoxetine) 88
Serax (oxazepam) 5
Seroquel (quetiapine) 56, 66, 70,
    79, 91, 94, 96, 107, 110
sertraline. See Zoloft Serzone
    (nefazodone) 104
Sonata (zaleplon) 99, 102, 114,
    116, 118, 121, 133
Sparlon (modafinil) 23, 28, 31, 36
Strattera (atomoxetine) 23, 28, 33,
    36, 39

T

tacrine. See Cognex
Tenormin (atenolol) 3
Thorazine (chlorpromazine) 110
Tofranil (imipramine) 10
Topamax (topiramate) 139
Tranxene (clorazepate) 5
tranylcypromine. See Parnate
trazodone. See Desyrel
triazolam. See Halcion

V

Valium (diazepam) 5
venlafaxine. See Effexor
Verapamil (calcium channel
    blocker) 72
Vivitrex (naltrexone depot) 139

W

Wellbutrin (bupropion) 36, 60, 63,
    73, 84, 104, 141

X

Xanax (alprazolam) 3, 5, 20, 116,
    137

Z

zaleplon. See Sonata
ziprasidone. See Geodon
Zofran (ondansetron) 139
Zoloft (sertraline) 3, 10, 14, 16, 19,
    48, 51, 60, 63, 84, 88, 98, 101
zolpidem. See Ambien
Zyban (bupropion) 141
Zyprexa (olanzapine) 48, 56, 66, 70,
    79, 91, 107, 110

Notes

Thank you!

Thank you for reading 40 Cases.
I hope you found this book interesting and helpful.
Please visit Dr. Lundt's
Website at
www.leslielundt.com

You can download medication consent
forms and a sleep questionnaire directly
from this Website.

Other books by Leslie Lundt MD
You Can Think Like a Psychiatrist
An overview of psychotropic medications

Psychopharmacology of Addiction (coming soon)